easy to make!
Chocolate

Good Housekeeping

easy to make!
Chocolate

COLLINS & BROWN

First published in Great Britain in 2009
by Collins & Brown
10 Southcombe Street
London W14 0RA

An imprint of Anova Books Company Ltd

The Good Housekeeping website is
www.allaboutyou.com/goodhousekeeping

1 2 3 4 5 6 7 8 9

ISBN 978-184340-494-1

A catalogue record for this book is available from the
British Library.

Repro by Dot Gradations UK, Ltd
Printed by Times Offset, Malaysia

This book can be ordered direct from the publisher. Contact the
marketing department, but try your bookshop first.

www.anovabooks.com

NOTES

- Both metric and imperial measures are given for the recipes. Follow either set of measures, not a mixture of both, as they are not interchangeable.
- All spoon measures are level.
  1 tsp = 5ml spoon; 1 tbsp = 15ml spoon.
- Ovens and grills must be preheated to the specified temperature.
- Use sea salt and freshly ground black pepper unless otherwise suggested.
- Fresh herbs should be used unless dried herbs are specified in a recipe.
- Medium eggs should be used except where otherwise specified. Free-range eggs are recommended.
- Note that certain recipes contain raw or lightly cooked eggs. The young, elderly, pregnant women and anyone with an immune-deficiency disease should avoid these, because of the slight risk of salmonella.
- Calorie, fat and carbohydrate counts per serving are provided for the recipes.

Picture credits
Photographers: Martin Brigdale (33, 42, 43, 45, 47, 48, 55, 56, 58, 59, 60, 62, 63, 64, 68, 69, 70, 75, 77, 78, 80, 89, 95, 97, 98, 102, 108, 110, 111, 115, 120, 121, 123, 125, 126); Nicky Dowey (pages 8–29, 34, 35, 36, 37, 38, 40, 41, 46, 49, 52, 57, 82, 83, 84, 85, 87, 88, 91, 100, 103, 105, 107, 116, 117, 118, 122); Steve Baxter (page 53); Craig Robertson (pages 65, 67, 76, 79, 90, 96, 99, 106)

Contents

Foreword

There are times when only chocolate will do. I love a small dark square after I've polished off supper on those occasions when I'm still left wanting more. Allowing it to release its deep flavours slowly on the tongue – chocolate melts at body temperature – is the best way to appreciate this wonderful ingredient. Try it... you'll feel more satisfied so will only need to eat a little piece. Depending on what brand, it can taste rich and bitter – perfect with a cup of coffee... or more subtle with back notes of red wine. Team it with something soft and spicy, such as a new world shiraz and you'll have a marriage made in heaven.

I also like to keep a good stash of dark chocolate in the cupboard to use in recipes whenever I need to. However, if that's too much of a temptation and you find your stores are running low, freeze it. I've discovered it's very easy to forget about something that's hidden away in there. It'll come to no harm and you can use it straight from frozen.

No matter what you make though, adding chocolate will always feel indulgent. A simple sauce made with cream and milk, dark or white turns fresh fruit and ice cream into a treat. If I'm in the mood for something more decadent – a show-stopping finale to a lovely meal with friends, I'll pick something like the Chocolate and Cherry Amaretti Tart on page 87. It ticks all the boxes for me – I love the combination of pastry, fruit and chocolate and it'll look stunning finished with a final dusting of icing sugar. It's also fun and easy to make. Knowing that it's been triple tested, like all the recipes here, means it'll look and taste fabulous the very first time I make it, too.

Enjoy!

Emma

Emma Marsden
Cookery Editor
Good Housekeeping

0

The Basics

Type of chocolate to use

Chocolate is available in many different forms, from cocoa powder to bars of plain, milk, white and dark, bitter chocolate.

The type of chocolate you choose will have a dramatic effect on the end product. For the best results, buy chocolate that has a high proportion of cocoa solids, preferably at least 70 per cent. Most supermarkets stock a selection. Chocolate with a high percentage of cocoa solids has a rich flavour and is perfect for sauces, ganache (see opposite), most sweets, cakes and puddings. Avoid chocolate-flavoured imitations of the real thing at all costs.

At the top end of the scale, couverture chocolate is the one preferred by chefs for confectionery work and gives an intense chocolate flavour that is probably best reserved for special mousses and gâteaux. It is available in milk, plain and white varieties from specialist chocolate shops and websites.

Using chocolate

As well as being a delicious ingredient in many cakes and bakes, chocolate can be used for wonderful puddings, for dipping fruit in, and for making sauces and stunning decorations.

Melting

For cooking or making decorations, chocolate is usually melted first.

1 Break the chocolate into pieces and put in a heatproof bowl or in the top of a double boiler. Set over a pan of gently simmering water, making sure the base of the bowl doesn't touch the water.

2 Heat very gently until the chocolate starts to melt, then stir only once or twice until completely melted.

Chocolate sauce

1 Chop the best-quality dark chocolate (with a minimum of 70 per cent cocoa solids) and put it into a saucepan with 50ml (2fl oz) water per 100g (3½oz) chocolate.

2 Heat slowly, allowing the chocolate to melt, then stir until the sauce is smooth. To liven up this simple chocolate sauce, see the variations below.

Variations

These are all suitable for a sauce made with 200g (7oz) chocolate:

Milk or single cream Substituted in whole or in part for the water.

Coffee Stir in a teaspoon of instant coffee or a shot of espresso when melting the chocolate.

Spices Add a pinch of ground cinnamon, crushed cardamom seeds or freshly grated nutmeg to the melting chocolate.

Vanilla extract Stir in ¼ tsp vanilla when melting the chocolate.

Rum, whisky or cognac Stir in about 1 tsp alcohol when melting the chocolate.

Butter Stir in 25g (1oz) towards the end of heating.

Ganache

This filling, topping and glaze is made from good-quality chocolate mixed with cream and butter. Depending on what the ganache is being used for, liqueurs or flavourings can be added. Increasing the ratio of cream to chocolate will make the ganache lighter, and butter adds shine.

Ganache can also be used to fill chocolates and in puddings. The recipe on page 122 (step 2 of Nutty Chocolate Truffles) is very versatile.

Cook's Tips

When melting chocolate, always use a gentle heat.
Make sure the base of the bowl is not touching the water.
However tempting, only stir the chocolate once or twice until it has melted: over-stirring will make it thicken into a sticky mess.
Don't let water or steam touch the chocolate or it will 'seize' – become hard and unworkable. If it has seized, you can try saving it by stirring in a few drops of flavourless vegetable oil.

Shaving

This is the easiest decoration of all because it doesn't call for melting the chocolate.

1 Hold a chocolate bar upright on the worksurface and shave pieces off the edge with a swivel peeler.

2 Alternatively, grate the chocolate against a coarse or medium-coarse grater, to make very fine shavings.

Decorative uses

When preparing chocolate for decorative uses, work quickly so that the chocolate does not set hard before you have finished.

Chocolate curls

1 Melt the chocolate (see page 10) and spread it out in a thin layer on a marble slab or clean worksurface. Leave to firm up.

2 Using a sharp blade (such as a pastry scraper, a cook's knife or a very stiff spatula) draw it through the chocolate at a 45° angle. The size of the curls will be determined by the width of the blade.

Chocolate leaves

1 Wash and dry some rose or bay leaves. Spread slightly cooled melted chocolate in a thin, even layer over the shiny side of the leaf. Spread it right out to the edge using a paintbrush, but wipe off any chocolate that drips over the edge.

2 Leave to cool completely. Then, working very gently and carefully, peel the leaf off the chocolate.

Chocolate wafers

1 Cut a piece of greaseproof paper to the required width. Brush the paper evenly with melted chocolate and leave until the chocolate has almost set.

2 Using a knife, cut the chocolate (while still on the paper) into pieces (straight or curved, square or triangular, narrow or wide). You can also cut out chocolate shapes using small cutters. Leave to cool and harden completely, either on the worksurface (for flat wafers) or draped over a rolling pin (for curled). Carefully peel the wafers off the paper, handling them as little as possible, and store in the refrigerator for up to 24 hours.

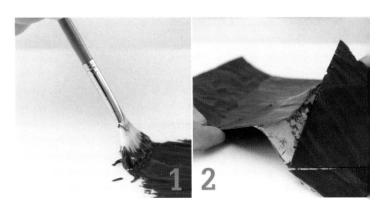

Piping

1 Draw your designs on a sheet of white paper, then lay a sheet of greaseproof paper on top.

2 Take a piping cone or piping bag fitted with a fine nozzle and fill with melted chocolate (see page 10).

3 Using light, even pressure, pipe chocolate on to the paper following the outline of the drawing. Leave to set, then carefully remove the piped lines using a fine-bladed knife.

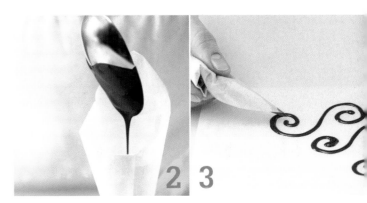

Hot Chocolate

To serve six, you will need:
125g (4oz) plain chocolate, grated, 450ml (³/₄ pint) milk, 1 tbsp cornflour, 4 tbsp golden caster sugar, 140ml (4¹/₂fl oz) double cream.

1 Put the grated chocolate and half the milk into a pan and heat gently until the chocolate has melted. Put the cornflour into a bowl and slowly add the remaining milk, stirring well to mix thoroughly. Add the cornflour mix to the pan and whisk it into the melted chocolate, then stir in the sugar. Cook on a low heat for 3 minutes, whisking constantly, until the hot chocolate thickens. Remove the pan from the heat and continue to whisk the chocolate until smooth.

2 Whisk the cream until thick. Pour the hot chocolate into six cups, top with cream and serve.

Baking

You don't need much specialist equipment for making cakes and cookies; in fact, you probably have many of thes items listed here in your kitchen already.

Weighing and measuring

Scales

Accurate measurement is essential when baking. The most accurate scale is the electronic type, capable of weighing up to 2kg (4½lb) or 5kg (11lb) in increments of 1–5g. Buy one with a flat platform on which you can put your own bowl or measuring jug, and always remember to set the scale to zero before adding the ingredients.

Measuring jugs

These can be plastic or glass, and are available in sizes ranging from 500ml (18fl oz) to 2 litres (3½ pints), or even 3 litres (5¼ pints). Have two – a large one and a small one – marked with both metric and imperial measurements.

Measuring cups

Commonly used in the US, these are for measuring liquid and dry ingredients. Cups are bought in sets of ¼, ⅓, ½ and 1 cup. A standard 1-cup measure is equivalent to about 250ml (9fl oz).

Measuring spoons

Useful for the smallest units, accurate spoon measurements go from 1.25ml (¼ tsp) to 15ml (1 tbsp).

Mixing

Bowls

For mixing large quantities, such as cake mixtures, you will need at least two large bowls, including one with a diameter of up to 38cm (15in).
• Plastic or glass bowls are best if you need to use them in the microwave.
• Steel bowls with a rubber foot will keep their grip on the worksurface.

Spoons

For general mixing, the cheap and sturdy wooden spoon still can't be beaten, but equivalents made from thermoplastic materials are heatproof and may suit you better. A large metal spoon for folding ingredients together is also invaluable.

Bakeware

As well as being thin enough to conduct heat quickly and efficiently, bakeware should be sturdy enough not to warp when heated. Most bakeware is made from aluminium, and it may have enamel or non-stick coatings.

Cake tins Available in many shapes and sizes, tins may be single-piece, loose-based or springform.
Loaf tins Available in various sizes; one of the most useful is a 900g (2lb) tin.
Pie tins and muffin tins You should have both single-piece tins and loose-based tins for flans and pies.
Oven-safe silicone is safe to touch straight from the oven, is inherently non-stick and is also flexible – making it easy to remove muffins and other bakes.

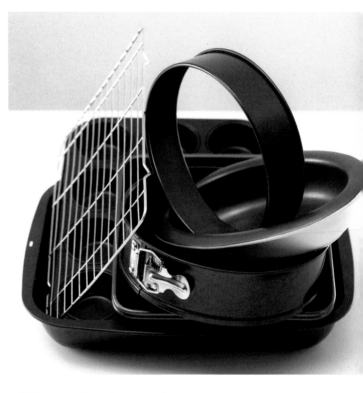

Electrical equipment

Food processor For certain tasks, such as making breadcrumbs or pastry, or for chopping large quantities of nuts, a food processor is unbeatable. Most come with a number of attachments – dough hooks, graters, slicers – which are worth having, even if only for occasional use.
Blender This is less versatile than a food processor, but unmatched for certain tasks, such as puréeing fruit. The traditional jug blender is great but some cooks prefer a hand-held stick blender, which can be used directly in a pan, bowl or jug.
Freestanding mixer An electric mixer may be a good investment if you do a lot of baking, but decide first whether you have space in your kitchen. It is big and heavy to store.
Electric hand mixer Useful for creaming together butter and sugar in baking and for making meringues. It doesn't take up a lot of space and can be packed away easily.

Other useful utensils

Baking sheets (two)	Cooling racks (two)
Spatulas	Palette knife
Wire whisks	Ruler
Fine sieve	Dredger
Microplane grater	Serrated knife
Rolling pin	Icing bag and piping
Thin skewers	nozzles
Cookie cutters	Vegetable peeler

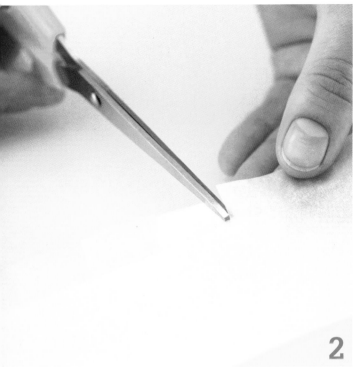

Lining tins

When making cakes, you usually need to grease and/or line the tin with greaseproof paper before filling it with cake mixture. Lightly grease the tin first to help keep the paper in place. You will need to use different techniques according to the shape of the tin.

Round tin

1 Put the tin on a sheet of greaseproof paper and draw a circle around its circumference. Cut out the circle just inside the drawn line.

2 Cut a strip or strips about 2cm ($^3/_4$in) wider than the depth of the tin and fold up one long edge of each strip by 1cm ($^1/_2$in). Make cuts, about 2.5cm (1in) apart, through the folded edge of the strip(s) up to the fold line.

3 Lightly grease the tin with butter, making sure it is completely coated.

4 Press the strip(s) on to the sides of the tin so that the snipped edge sits on the base.

5 Lay the circle in the bottom of the tin and grease the paper.

Swiss roll tin

Use this method for Swiss roll or other shallow baking tins.

1 Lightly grease the tin with butter, making sure it is completely coated.

2 Cut a piece of baking parchment into a rectangle 7.5cm (3in) wider and longer than the tin. Press it into the tin and cut at the corners, then fold to fit neatly. Grease all over.

Loaf tin

1 Lightly grease the tin with butter, making sure it is completely coated.

2 Cut a sheet of greaseproof paper to the same length as the base, and wide enough to cover both the base and the long sides. Press it into position, making sure that it sits snugly in the corners.

3 Now cut another sheet to the same width as the base and long enough to cover both the base and the ends of the tin. Press into place. Grease the paper all over.

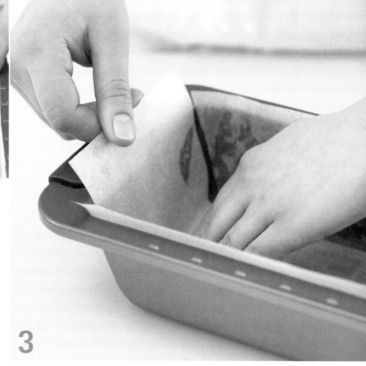

3

Square tin

1 Cut out a square of greaseproof paper slightly smaller than the base of the tin. Cut four strips about 2cm (³/₄in) wider than the depth of the tin and fold up one of the longest edges of each strip by 1cm (¹/₂in).

2 Lightly grease the tin with butter, making sure it is coated on all sides and in the corners.

3 Cut one strip to the length of the side of the tin and press into place in one corner, then along the length of the strip with the narrow folded section sitting on the base. Continue, cutting to fit into the corners, to cover all four sides.

4 Lay the square on the base of the tin, then grease the paper, taking care not to move the side strips.

Perfect lining

Use greaseproof paper for all cakes, and baking parchment for roulades and meringues.
Apply the butter with a small piece of greaseproof paper.
Don't grease too thickly – this 'fries' the edges of the cake.

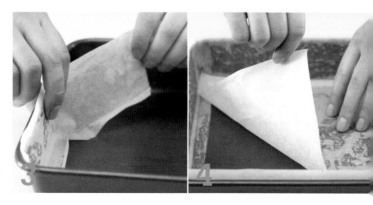

Creaming

Use for a classic creamed (Victoria) sponge.

1 Beat the butter and sugar with an electric whisk or wooden spoon until pale, soft and creamy.

2 Beat the eggs and gradually add to the butter and sugar mixture, beating well until the mixture is thick and of dropping consistency. You can add a spoonful of flour while adding the eggs, to prevent curdling.

3 Gently fold in the flour using a large metal spoon or spatula, then spoon the mixture into the prepared tin(s), level the surface and bake.

Making cakes

Home-made cakes are always welcome – especially chocolate ones. Most cakes use one of these basic techniques: creaming, all-in-one or whisking.

All-in-one

1 Put the butter, sugar, eggs, flour and baking powder in a large bowl or mixer. Using an electric hand mixer, mix slowly to start, then increase the speed slightly until well combined. Fold in any remaining ingredients then spoon into the prepared tin(s) and bake.

Whisking

1 Melt the butter in a small pan. Put the eggs and sugar in a large bowl set over a pan of simmering water. Whisk for about 5 minutes with an electric hand mixer until creamy and pale and the mixture leaves a trail when you lift the whisk.

2 Gently fold half the flour into the mixture. Pour the butter around the edge of the mixture, then fold in the remaining flour and butter. Pour into the prepared tin(s) and bake.

Testing a sponge

1 Gently press the centre of the sponge. It should feel springy. If it's a whisked cake, it should be just shrinking away from the sides of the tin.

2 If you have to put it back into the oven, close the door gently so that the vibrations don't cause the cake to sink in the centre.

Splitting and filling a cake

1 Allow the cake to cool completely before splitting.

2 Use a knife with a thin blade such as a bread knife. Cut a notch from top to bottom on one side so you will know where to line the pieces up. Cut midway between top and bottom, about 30 per cent of the way through the cake. Turn the cake while cutting, taking care to keep the blade parallel with the base, until you have cut all the way around.

3 Continue cutting until you have cut through the central core; then carefully lift off the top of the cake.

4 Warm the filling slightly to make it easier to spread, then spread over the base, stopping 1cm (½in) from the edge.

5 Carefully put the top layer of cake on top of the filling and gently pat into place.

Buttercream Icing

To cover the top of a 20.5cm (8in) cake, you will need:
75g (3oz) unsalted butter, 175g (6oz) icing sugar, sifted, a few drops of vanilla extract, 1–2 tbsp milk.

1 Soften the butter in a mixing bowl, then beat until light and fluffy.

2 Gradually stir in the remaining ingredients and beat until smooth.

Variations

Chocolate Blend 1 tbsp cocoa powder with 2 tbsp boiling water. Cool, then add to the mixture in place of the milk.
Citrus Replace the vanilla with a little orange, lemon or lime zest, and use some of the fruit's juice in place of the milk.

Making cheesecakes

There are many ways to make this perennial favourite, which can be baked or simply chilled and set with gelatine. When baking cheesecakes, watch the temperature – too high a heat can cause the top to crack.

Chilled cheesecake

An uncooked cheesecake is usually set with gelatine and made with a mixture of cream cheese and perhaps some cottage cheese flavoured with lemon zest. The mixture is poured on to a biscuit crumb base (usually made with crushed biscuits mixed with melted butter) that has been pressed into a flan tin then chilled until firm. The whole cheesecake is then chilled to set. Fresh fruit or a fruit coulis can be added as a topping.

Baked Chocolate Cheesecake

To serve 12, you will need:
200g (7oz) pack Bourbon biscuits, 50g (2oz) melted butter, 200g (7oz) chopped milk chocolate, 2 x 250g (9oz) tubs mascarpone cheese, 2 x 200g (7oz) tubs ricotta cheese, 4 large eggs, 100g (3½oz) caster sugar, 2–3 drops vanilla extract, cocoa-dusted almonds, cocoa for dusting, crème fraîche to serve.

1   Line a 20.5cm (8in) springform tin with non-stick baking parchment. Whizz the biscuits in a processor to crumbs, then mix in the melted butter. Tip into the tin and press down using the back of a spoon. Chill for 1 hour.

2   Preheat the oven to 180°C (fan 160°C) mark 4. Melt the chocolate in a heatproof bowl over a pan of gently simmering water, making sure the base of the bowl doesn't touch the water. Remove from the heat and leave to cool a little.

3   In a large bowl, beat together the mascarpone and ricotta cheeses, eggs, sugar, vanilla extract and melted chocolate. Spoon over the biscuit base and bake for 1–1¼ hours, or until golden on top but slightly wobbly in the centre. Turn off the oven, leave the door ajar and leave the cheesecake inside to cool.

4   When cooled, decorate with cocoa-dusted almonds, dust with cocoa and serve with crème fraîche. Cut into slices to serve.

Making batters

Batters can serve a number of purposes, and are remarkably versatile for something so simple. All you need to remember when working with them is to mix quickly and lightly.

Pancakes

To make 8 pancakes, you will need:
125g (4oz) plain flour, a pinch of salt, 1 egg, 300ml (½ pint) milk, oil and butter to fry.

1 Sift the flour and salt, make a well in the middle and whisk in the egg. Work in the milk, then leave to stand for 20 minutes. Heat a pan and coat lightly with fat. Coat thinly with batter.

2 Cook for 1½–2 minutes until golden, turning carefully turning once.

White Chocolate and Berry Crêpes

To serve 4, you will need:
1 quantity of basic pancake mixture (above), 500g bag frozen mixed berries, thawed, 150g (5oz) good-quality white chocolate, broken into pieces, 150ml (¼ pint) carton double cream.

1 Make the pancake mixture as above and leave to stand for 20 minutes.

2 Put the berries into a large pan, place over a medium heat and cook for 5 minutes until heated through.

3 Put the chocolate and cream in a heatproof bowl over a pan of simmering water (making sure the bottom of the bowl doesn't touch the hot water). Heat gently, stirring, for 5 minutes or until the chocolate is just melted. Remove bowl from the pan and mix the chocolate and cream to a smooth sauce.

4 Meanwhile, cook the pancakes and keep warm interleaved with greaseproof paper. To serve, put two pancakes on each warm plate and fold each in half. Spoon an eighth of the berries into the middle of each crêpe. Fold over the filling and pour the hot chocolate sauce over the top. Serve at once.

Making meringues

Sweet and simple to make, meringues have just two ingredients: egg whites and sugar. Home-made meringues have a lovely freshness that's often lacking in store-bought ones. Stored in an airtight container, they will keep well for several weeks.

Simple meringues

For 12 meringues, you will need:
3 egg whites, 175g (6oz) caster sugar.

1 Preheat the oven to 170°C (150°C fan oven) mark 3. Cover a baking sheet with baking parchment.

2 Put the egg whites in a large, clean bowl. Whisk them until soft peaks form. Add a spoonful of sugar and whisk until glossy.

3 Keep adding the sugar a spoonful at a time, whisking thoroughly after each addition, until you have used half the sugar. The mixture should be thick and glossy.

4 Sprinkle the remaining sugar over the mixture and then gently fold in using a metal spoon.

5 Hold a dessertspoon in each hand and pick up a spoonful of mixture in one spoon, then scrape the other one against it to lift the mixture off. Repeat the process a few times, to form a rough oval

Perfect meringues

- Meringues are best baked in the evening, or whenever you know you won't be needing your oven for a good few hours, as they must be left to dry in the turned-off oven for several hours.
- Get a pan of water simmering gently before you start making the meringues, and line a large baking sheet with greaseproof paper or a silicone baking mat.
- Make sure the mixing bowl is spotlessly clean, as the tiniest trace of grease can keep the whites from whisking up properly. Also, check that your electric whisk is absolutely clean.
- If using a free-standing mixer with a whisk attachment, rather than a hand-held whisk, put the bowl of the mixer over the pan of simmering water. Dry it off and return it to the mixer stand.
- Don't rush the whisking process. If the egg whites are not beaten for long enough, they won't hold their shape when baked.

shape. Using the empty spoon, push the oval on to the baking sheet; hold it just over the sheet so that it doesn't drop from a great height. Continue this process with the remaining mixture to make 12 meringues.

6 Put the meringues in the oven and bake for 15 minutes, then turn the oven off and leave them in the oven to dry out overnight.

Variations

- For a richer flavour, add 1 tsp vanilla extract or 50g (2oz) ground almonds or toasted hazelnuts.
- You can add a tiny amount of food colouring to make them a pale pink, lilac, and so on.
- Shape the meringues using a pastry bag instead of dessertspoons, if you like.
- Poaching the meringues keeps them soft throughout, perfect for serving on a pool of custard to make Floating Islands. To poach meringues, form them into ovals using two soup spoons and poach in a pan of simmering water for about 3 minutes.

Making soufflés

Light, fluffy soufflés made with whisked egg whites folded into a richly flavoured egg custard may be sweet or savoury. For a perfectly risen soufflé, use a traditional straight-sided soufflé dish.
For perfect soufflés:

- Run a knife around the inside of the dish before baking to help achieve the classic 'hat' effect.
- Ensure you have a well-flavoured (or well-seasoned) sauce, because the egg white will dilute the flavour.
- When you fold the sauce and egg whites together, work very gently to avoid knocking the air out of the egg whites.

Making roulades

A roulade is made from a very light cake mixture and does not contain flour. It remains very soft when baked, and can therefore be rolled easily. Spread with a filling such as jam and cream first.

Variation

To add whipped cream to a roulade, cool the roulade first. To do this, turn out the roulade on to baking parchment. Do not remove the lining paper, but roll the roulade while still warm. Leave to cool, unroll and peel off the paper. Spread with cream, and jam if you wish, and re-roll.

Chocolate Cherry Roll

To serve 8, you will need:
4 tbsp cocoa powder, plus extra to dust, 150ml (¼ pint) milk, 5 eggs, separated, 125g (4oz) golden caster sugar, 1–2 tbsp cherry jam, warmed, 400g (14oz) can pitted cherries, drained, sifted icing sugar to dust.

1 Preheat the oven to 180°C (160°C fan oven) mark 4 and line a 30.5 x 20.5cm (12 x 8in) Swiss roll tin with baking parchment. Mix the cocoa with 3 tbsp milk in a bowl. Heat the remaining milk until almost boiling. Pour over the cocoa, stirring. Cool for 10 minutes.

2 Whisk the egg whites until soft peaks form. In another bowl, whisk the yolks with the sugar until pale and thick, then gradually whisk in the cooled milk. Fold in the egg whites, spoon the mixture into the tin, and level. Bake for 25 minutes until just firm.

3 Turn out on to a board lined with baking parchment and peel off the lining paper. Cover with a damp teatowel for a few minutes. Spread the jam over the roulade and top with the cherries. Very carefully, roll up from the shortest end. Dust with cocoa and icing sugar and serve in slices.

Chocolate Refrigerator Roll

There is no baking required.
To make 14 slices, you will need:

75g (3oz) digestive biscuits, 50g (2oz) flaked almonds, lightly toasted, 50g (2oz) ready-to-eat dried apricots, finely chopped, 1 piece preserved stem ginger in syrup, drained and finely chopped, 75g (3oz) white chocolate, roughly chopped, 175g (6oz) plain chocolate, in pieces, 65g (2¹/₂oz) unsalted butter, 50g (2oz) white chocolate, melted, to decorate.

1   Break the biscuits into chunky pieces and mix with the almonds, apricots, ginger and white chocolate.

2   Melt the plain chocolate with the butter in a heatproof bowl over a pan of gently simmering water, stirring occasionally, until smooth. Remove from the heat and leave until cool, but not beginning to set.

3   Pour the chocolate on to the biscuit mixture and stir gently to mix.

4   Spoon on to greaseproof paper and wrap this around the mixture, making a sausage about 20.5cm (8in) long. Chill for 1–2 hours until firm.

5   Cut the roll into 1cm (¹/₂in) slices.

6   Place slices on a clean sheet of greaseproof paper. Using a teaspoon, drizzle lines of melted white chocolate over to decorate. Chill until ready to serve.

Cook's Tip

Always make sure that the melted chocolate is quite cool before you mix it with the other ingredients, or the white chocolate will melt.

Making ice cream

Rich and creamy, fresh and fruity or sweet and indulgent, ice creams are easy to make and are the perfect accompaniment to many puddings, or can simply be enjoyed on their own.

Vanilla Ice Cream

To serve 4–6, you will need:
300ml (½ pint) milk, 1 vanilla pod, split lengthways,
3 egg yolks, 75g (3oz) golden caster sugar,
300ml (½ pint) double cream.

1 Put the milk and vanilla in a pan. Heat slowly until almost boiling. Cool for 20 minutes, then remove the vanilla pod. In a large bowl, whisk the egg yolks and sugar until thick and creamy. Gradually whisk in the milk, then strain back into the pan.

2 Cook over a low heat, stirring with a wooden spoon, until thick enough to coat the back of the spoon – do not boil. Pour into a chilled bowl and leave to cool.

3 Whisk the cream into the custard. Pour into an ice-cream maker and freeze or churn according to the manufacturer's instructions, or make by hand. Store in a covered freezerproof container; it will keep for up to two months. Put the ice cream in the refrigerator for 15–20 minutes before serving to soften slightly.

Making ice cream by hand

1 If possible, set the freezer to fast-freeze 1 hour ahead. Pour the ice-cream mixture into a shallow freezerproof container, cover and freeze until partially frozen.

2 Spoon into a bowl and mash with a fork to break up the ice crystals. Return to the container and freeze for another 2 hours. Repeat and freeze for another 3 hours.

Pitting cherries

A cherry stoner will remove the stones neatly, but it is important to position the fruit correctly.

1 First, remove the stems from the cherries, then wash the fruit and pat dry on kitchen paper. Put each cherry on the stoner with the stem end facing up. Close the stoner and gently press the handles together so that the metal rod pushes through the fruit, pressing out the stone.

2 If you do not have a cherry stoner, cut the cherries in half and remove the stones with the tip of a small pointed knife.

Using fruit

Citrus fruit is an important flavouring: the grated zest and juice of oranges and lemons are used in many cake mixtures and icings. Other fruit may be used as an ingredient or a colourful, fresh-tasting decoration.

Hulling strawberries

1 Wash the strawberries gently and dry on kitchen paper.

2 Remove the hull (the centre part that was attached to the plant) from the strawberry using a strawberry huller or a small, sharp knife. Put the knife into the hard area beneath the green stalk and gently rotate to remove a small, cone-shaped piece.

Zesting

Most citrus fruit is sprayed with wax and fungicides or pesticides. Unless you buy unwaxed fruit, wash it with a tiny drop of washing-up liquid and warm water, then rinse with clean water and dry thoroughly on kitchen paper.
To use a grater, rub the fruit over the grater, using a medium pressure to remove the zest without removing the white pith, which can be bitter.
To use a zester, press the blade into the citrus skin and run it along the surface to take off long shreds.

Food storage and hygiene

Storing food properly and preparing food in a hygienic way is important to ensure that food remains as nutritious and flavourful as possible, and to reduce the risk of food poisoning.

Hygiene

When you are preparing food, always follow these important guidelines:

Wash your hands thoroughly before handling food and again between handling different types of food, such as raw and cooked meat and poultry. If you have any cuts or grazes on your hands, be sure to keep them covered with a waterproof plaster.

Wash down worksurfaces regularly with a mild detergent solution or multi-surface cleaner.

Use a dishwasher if available. Otherwise, wear rubber gloves for washing up, so that the water temperature can be hotter than unprotected hands can bear. Change drying-up cloths and cleaning cloths regularly. Note that leaving dishes to drain is more hygienic than drying them with a teatowel.

Keep pets out of the kitchen if possible; or make sure they stay away from worksurfaces. Never allow animals on to worksurfaces.

Shopping

Always choose fresh ingredients, in prime condition, from stores and markets that have a regular turnover of stock to ensure you buy the freshest produce possible.

Make sure items are within their 'best before' or 'use by' date. (Foods with a long shelf life have a 'best before' date; more perishable items have a 'use by' date.)

Pack frozen and chilled items in an insulated cool bag at the checkout and put them into the freezer or refrigerator as soon as yo u get home.

During warm weather in particular, buy perishable foods just before you return home. When packing items at the checkout, sort them according to where you will store them when you get home – the refrigerator, freezer, storecupboard, vegetable rack, fruit bowl, etc. This will make unpacking easier – and quicker.

The storecupboard

Although storecupboard ingredients will generally last a long time, correct storage is important:

Always check packaging for storage advice, even with familiar foods, because storage requirements may change if additives, sugar or salt have been reduced. Check storecupboard foods for their 'best before' or 'use by' date and do not use them if the date has passed.

Keep all food cupboards scrupulously clean and make sure food containers and packets are properly sealed.

Once opened, treat canned foods as though fresh. Always transfer the contents to a clean container, cover and keep in the refrigerator. Similarly, jars, sauce bottles and cartons should be kept chilled after opening. (Check the label for safe storage times after opening.)

Transfer dry goods such as sugar, rice and pasta to moisture-proof containers. When supplies are used up, wash the container well and dry thoroughly before refilling with new supplies.

Store oils in a dark cupboard away from any heat source, as heat and light can make them turn rancid and affect their colour. For the same reason, buy olive oil in dark green bottles.

Store vinegars in a cool place; they can turn bad in a warm environment.

Store dried herbs, spices and flavourings in a cool, dark cupboard or in dark jars. Buy in small quantities as their flavour will not last indefinitely.

Store flours and sugars in airtight containers.

Refrigerator storage

Fresh food needs to be kept in the cool temperature of the refrigerator to keep it in good condition and discourage the growth of harmful bacteria. Store day-to-day perishable items, such as opened jams and jellies, mayonnaise and bottled sauces, in the refrigerator along with eggs and dairy products, fruit juices, bacon, fresh and cooked meat (on separate shelves), and salads and vegetables (except potatoes, which don't suit being stored in the cold). A refrigerator should be kept at an operating temperature of 4–5°C.

It is worth investing in a refrigerator thermometer to ensure that the correct temperature is maintained. To ensure the refrigerator is functioning effectively for safe food storage, follow these guidelines:

To avoid bacterial cross-contamination, store cooked and raw foods on separate shelves, putting cooked foods on the top shelf. Ensure that all items are well wrapped.

Never put hot food into the refrigerator, as this will cause the internal temperature of the refrigerator to rise.

Avoid overfilling the refrigerator, as this restricts the circulation of air and prevents the appliance from working properly.

It can take some time for the refrigerator to return to the correct operating temperature once the door has been opened, so don't leave it open any longer than is necessary.

Clean the refrigerator regularly, using a specially formulated germicidal refrigerator cleaner. Alternatively, use a weak solution of bicarbonate of soda: 1 tbsp to 1 litre (1³/₄ pints) water.

If the refrigerator doesn't have an automatic defrost facility, defrost regularly.

For pre-packed foods, always adhere to the 'use by' date on the packet.

1

Cakes and Brownies

Chocolate Victoria Sandwich

175g (6oz) unsalted butter, softened, plus extra to grease

3 tbsp cocoa powder

175g (6oz) golden caster sugar

3 medium eggs, beaten

160g (5½oz) self-raising flour, sifted

golden caster sugar to dredge

For the chocolate buttercream

1 tbsp cocoa powder

75g (3oz) unsalted butter, softened

175g (6oz) icing sugar, sifted

a few drops of vanilla extract

1–2 tbsp milk or water

1 Preheat the oven to 190°C (170°C fan oven) mark 5. Grease two 18cm (7in) sandwich tins and line the base of each with a round of baking parchment. Blend the cocoa powder with 3 tbsp hot water to a smooth paste and allow to cool.

2 Cream the butter and sugar together, using a free-standing mixer or electric whisk, until pale and fluffy. Add the cooled cocoa mixture and beat until evenly blended.

3 Add the beaten eggs, a little at a time, beating well after each addition. Fold in half of the flour, using a metal spoon or large spatula, then carefully fold in the rest.

4 Divide the mixture evenly between the tins and level the surface with a palette knife. Bake both cakes on the middle shelf of the oven for about 20 minutes or until well risen, springy to the touch and beginning to shrink away from the sides of the tins. Leave in the tins for 5 minutes, then turn out and cool on a wire rack.

5 To make the chocolate buttercream, blend the cocoa powder with 3 tbsp boiling water and set aside to cool. Put the butter into a bowl and beat with a wooden spoon until it is light and fluffy. Gradually stir in the icing sugar. Add the blended cocoa, vanilla extract and milk or water, and beat well until light and smooth.

6 When the cakes are cool, sandwich them together with the chocolate buttercream and sprinkle the top with caster sugar.

Get Ahead

This cake will keep well for up to one week if stored in an airtight tin in a cool larder.

Makes 8 Slices	EASY		NUTRITIONAL INFORMATION
	Preparation Time 20 minutes	**Cooking Time** 20 minutes, plus cooling	**Per Slice** 520 calories, 29.5g fat (of which 18.5g saturates), 61.7g carbohydrate, 1g salt

Decadent Chocolate Cake

225g (8oz) unsalted butter, softened, plus extra to grease

300g (11oz) plain chocolate (at least 70% cocoa solids), broken into pieces

225g (8oz) golden caster sugar

225g (8oz) ground almonds

8 large eggs, separated

125g (4oz) fresh brown breadcrumbs

For the ganache

175g (6oz) plain chocolate, broken into pieces

75g (3oz) unsalted butter, softened

4 tbsp double cream

1 Preheat the oven to 180°C (160°C fan oven) mark 4. Grease and line a 23cm (9in) springform cake tin.

2 Melt the chocolate in a heatproof bowl over a pan of gently simmering water. Remove the bowl from the pan. Put the butter and sugar into a large bowl and beat together until light and creamy. Add the ground almonds, egg yolks and breadcrumbs, and beat well. Slowly add the melted chocolate and carefully stir it in, taking care not to over-mix, as the chocolate may seize up.

3 Put the egg whites into a clean, grease-free bowl and whisk until they form soft peaks. Add half the whites to the chocolate mixture and fold in lightly using a large metal spoon, then carefully fold in the remainder. Pour the mixture into the prepared tin and level the surface. Bake for 1 hour 20 minutes or until a skewer inserted into the centre comes out clean. Leave in the tin for 5 minutes, then transfer to a wire rack for 2–3 hours to cool completely.

4 To make the ganache, put the chocolate, butter and double cream into a heatproof bowl over a pan of gently simmering water. Leave to melt, then stir until smooth. Pour the ganache over the centre of the cake and spread it with a palette knife. Leave to set.

Serves 12	A LITTLE EFFORT		NUTRITIONAL INFORMATION
	Preparation Time 30 minutes	**Cooking Time** 1½ hours, plus cooling	**Per Serving** 693 calories, 49g fat (of which 23g saturates), 54g carbohydrate, 0.7g salt

Cook's Tip

To ice and finish the cake, put 175g (6oz) white chocolate in a heatproof bowl with 150ml (¼ pint) double cream and melt over a pan of gently simmering water until smooth. Cool slightly, beating the mixture until it thickens. Carefully remove the cake from the tin, gently easing away the paper, and spread over the icing. Chill to set. Decorate with milk or plain chocolate curls (see page 12).

White Chocolate Mousse Cake

125g (4oz) unsalted butter, softened, plus extra to grease

5 large eggs, separated

150g (5oz) caster sugar

225g (8oz) plain chocolate (at least 50% cocoa solids), broken into pieces, melted (see page 10) and left to cool slightly

milk or plain chocolate curls to decorate (see page 12)

For the mousse layer

4 large eggs, separated

225g (8oz) white chocolate, broken into pieces, melted (see page 10) and left to cool slightly

150ml (¼ pint) double cream

2 tsp powdered gelatine, sprinkled over 2 tbsp water in a small, heatproof bowl and left to soak for 10 minutes

1 Preheat the oven to 190°C (170°C fan oven) mark 5. Grease and line a 20.5cm (8in) springform cake tin. Whisk the five egg yolks with the sugar in a heatproof bowl over a pan of hot water until thick and creamy. Gradually beat in the butter until smooth. Off the heat, beat in the melted chocolate. Whisk the egg whites to soft peaks; fold into the chocolate mixture. Pour into the tin. Tap the tin to disperse bubbles. Bake for 50–55 minutes until risen and firm, covering with foil halfway through cooking. Leave to cool in the tin for 1 hour.

2 For the mousse, beat the four egg yolks into the chocolate, followed by the cream. Put the bowl of gelatine over a pan of simmering water until the gelatine dissolves. Whisk the egg whites to soft peaks. Stir the gelatine into the chocolate mixture. Stir in a spoonful of egg white; fold in the remainder. Remove the cake from the tin; split horizontally (see page 19). Line the tin with greaseproof paper. Put one round of cake in the base. Pour the mousse over it. Chill for 30 minutes. Put the remaining cake on top and chill overnight. Ice and finish the cake (see Cook's Tip).

FOR THE CONFIDENT COOK		NUTRITIONAL INFORMATION		Serves
Preparation Time 45 minutes, plus chilling	**Cooking Time** About 1 hour, plus cooling	**Per Serving** 433 calories, 31g fat (of which 18g saturates), 34g carbohydrate, 0.3g salt	Gluten free	**16**

125g (4oz) unsalted butter, softened

125g (4oz) light muscovado sugar

2 medium eggs, beaten

15g (½oz) cocoa powder

100g (3½oz) self-raising flour

100g (3½oz) plain chocolate (at least 70% cocoa solids), roughly chopped

Chocolate Cup Cakes

For the topping

150ml (¼ pint) double cream

100g (3½oz) plain chocolate
(at least 70% cocoa solids), broken up

1 Preheat the oven to 190°C (170°C fan oven) mark 5. Line bun tins or muffin pans with 18 paper muffin cases.

2 Beat together the butter and sugar until light and fluffy. Gradually beat in the eggs. Sift the cocoa powder with the flour and fold into the creamed mixture with the chopped chocolate.

3 Divide the mixture among the paper cases and lightly flatten the surface with the back of a spoon. Bake for 20 minutes. Cool in the cases.

4 For the topping, put the cream and chocolate into a heavy-based pan over a low heat and heat until melted, then allow to cool and thicken slightly. Spoon on to the cooled cakes and leave to set for 30 minutes.

	EASY		NUTRITIONAL INFORMATION
Makes **18**	**Preparation Time** 15 minutes	**Cooking Time** 20 minutes, plus cooling and setting	**Per Cake** 203 calories, 14g fat (of which 8g saturates), 19g carbohydrate, 0.2g salt

Cook's Tip

To make the frosted flowers, whisk 1 medium egg white in a clean bowl for 30 seconds until frothy. Brush it over 12 violet petals and put on a wire rack. Lightly dust with caster sugar and leave to dry.

Vanilla and White Chocolate Cup Cakes

125g (4oz) unsalted butter, at room temperature
125g (4oz) golden caster sugar
1 vanilla pod
2 medium eggs
125g (4oz) self-raising flour, sifted
1 tbsp vanilla extract
200g (7oz) white chocolate, broken into pieces
12 crystallised violets or frosted flowers (see Cook's Tip)

1 Preheat the oven to 190°C (170°C fan oven) mark 5. Line a bun tin or muffin pan with 12 paper muffin cases.

2 Put the butter and sugar in a bowl. Split the vanilla pod lengthways, scrape out the seeds and add to the bowl. Add the eggs, flour and vanilla extract, and beat thoroughly, using an electric whisk, until smooth and creamy. Spoon the mixture into the muffin cases and bake for 15–20 minutes until pale golden, risen and springy to the touch. Leave in the tin for 2–3 minutes, then transfer to a wire rack to cool.

3 Melt the chocolate in a heatproof bowl over a pan of gently simmering water. Stir until smooth and leave to cool slightly. Spoon the chocolate on to the cakes, top with a frosted flower and leave to set.

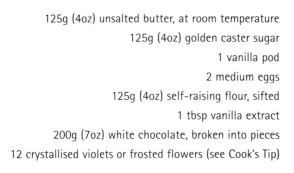

EASY		NUTRITIONAL INFORMATION	Makes
Preparation Time 25 minutes	**Cooking Time** 15–20 minutes, plus cooling	**Per Cake** 270 calories, 15g fat (of which 9g saturates), 32g carbohydrate, 0.2g salt	**12**

Lamingtons

125g (4oz) unsalted butter, softened, plus extra to grease

125g (4oz) golden caster sugar

2 medium eggs

125g (4oz) self-raising flour, sifted

1 tsp baking powder

2 tsp vanilla extract

For the topping

200g (7oz) icing sugar

50g (2oz) cocoa powder

25g (1oz) unsalted butter, cubed

5 tbsp milk

200g (7oz) desiccated coconut

1 Preheat the oven to 180°C (160°C fan oven) mark 4. Grease and line a 15cm (6in) square cake tin.

2 Put the butter into a large bowl and add the caster sugar, eggs, flour, baking powder and vanilla extract. Beat with an electric whisk until creamy. Turn the mixture into the prepared tin and level the surface. Bake for about 30 minutes or until just firm to the touch and a skewer inserted into the centre comes out clean. Transfer to a wire rack to cool. Wrap and store, overnight if possible, so that the cake is easier to slice.

3 To make the topping, sift the icing sugar and cocoa powder into a bowl. Put the butter and milk into a small pan and heat until the butter has just melted. Pour over the icing sugar and stir until smooth, adding 2–3 tbsp water to make a consistency that thickly coats the back of a spoon.

4 Trim the side crusts from the cake and cut into 16 squares. Put them on a wire rack with a sheet of greaseproof paper underneath to catch drips of icing. Scatter the coconut on a large plate. Pierce a piece of cake through the top crust and dip into the icing until coated, turning the cake gently. Transfer to the wire rack. Once you've coated half the pieces, roll them in the coconut and transfer to a plate. Repeat with the remainder and leave to set for a couple of hours before serving.

Cook's Tip

If towards the end of coating the chocolate topping mixture has thickened, thin it down with a drop of warm water and stir in carefully.

EASY		NUTRITIONAL INFORMATION	Makes
Preparation Time 40 minutes	**Cooking Time** 30 minutes, plus cooling and setting	**Per Cake** 273 calories, 17g fat (of which 12g saturates), 29g carbohydrate, 0.4g salt	**16**

Chocolate Fudge Brownies

butter to grease

125g (4oz) milk chocolate, broken into pieces

9 ready-to-eat prunes

200g (7oz) light muscovado sugar

3 large egg whites

1 tsp vanilla extract

75g (3oz) plain flour, sifted

50g (2oz) white chocolate, chopped

icing sugar to dust

1 Preheat the oven to 180°C (160°C fan oven) mark 4. Grease and baseline a shallow 15cm (6in) square cake tin. Melt the milk chocolate in a heatproof bowl over a pan of gently simmering water. Remove from the heat and leave to cool slightly.

2 Put the prunes in a food processor or blender with 100ml (3½fl oz) water and whiz for 2–3 minutes to make a purée. Add the muscovado sugar and whiz briefly to mix.

3 Put the egg whites into a clean, grease-free bowl and whisk until they form soft peaks.

4 Add the vanilla extract, prune mixture, flour, white chocolate and egg whites to the bowl of melted chocolate. Fold everything together gently. Pour the mixture into the prepared tin and bake for 1 hour or until firm to the touch.

5 Leave to cool in the tin. Turn out, dust with icing sugar and cut into 12 squares.

Makes 12	EASY		NUTRITIONAL INFORMATION
	Preparation Time 20 minutes	**Cooking Time** 1 hour, plus cooling	**Per Brownie** 174 calories, 5g fat (of which 3g saturates), 33g carbohydrate, 0.1g salt

The Ultimate Chocolate Brownies

200g (7oz) butter, plus extra to grease

400g (14oz) plain chocolate (at least 70% cocoa solids), broken into pieces

225g (8oz) light muscovado sugar

1 tsp vanilla extract

150g (5oz) pecan nuts, roughly chopped

25g (1oz) cocoa powder, sifted, plus extra to dust (optional)

75g (3oz) self-raising flour, sifted

3 large eggs, beaten

1 Preheat the oven to 170°C (150°C fan oven) mark 3. Grease a shallow 20.5cm (8in) square cake tin and line the base with baking parchment. Melt the butter and chocolate in a heatproof bowl over a pan of gently simmering water, stirring occasionally. Remove from the heat and stir in the sugar, vanilla extract, pecan nuts, cocoa powder, flour and eggs.

2 Turn the mixture into the prepared tin and level the surface with the back of a spoon. Bake for about 1¼ hours or until set on the surface but still soft underneath.

3 Leave to cool in the tin for 2 hours. Turn out, dust with sifted cocoa powder, if you like, and cut into squares. Eat cold or serve warm with ice cream.

EASY		NUTRITIONAL INFORMATION	Makes **16**
Preparation Time 15 minutes	**Cooking Time** 1 hour 20 minutes, plus 2 hours cooling	**Per Brownie** 257 calories, 11g fat (of which 6g saturates), 38g carbohydrate, 0.2g salt	

Chocolate Swiss Roll

3 large eggs
125g (4oz) golden caster sugar
125g (4oz) plain flour, less 1$\frac{1}{2}$ tbsp, sifted
1$\frac{1}{2}$ tbsp cocoa powder, sifted
golden caster sugar to sprinkle
chocolate buttercream (see page 19) or whipped cream
icing sugar to dust

1 Preheat the oven to 200°C (180°C fan oven) mark 6. Line a 33 x 23cm (13 x 9in) Swiss roll tin with baking parchment. Whisk the eggs and sugar in a heatproof bowl until well blended. Stand the bowl over a pan of hot water and whisk until light and creamy. Off the heat, whisk for 5 minutes or until the mixture is cool and thick. Fold in half the flour and cocoa powder. Fold in the remaining flour and cocoa. Lightly fold in 1 tbsp hot water. Pour into a prepared Swiss roll tin. Bake for 10–12 minutes until well risen and the cake springs back when lightly pressed. Sprinkle a sheet of greaseproof paper generously with caster sugar. Turn out the cake on to the paper and remove the lining paper. Trim off the crusty edges and cover the sponge with greaseproof paper. Roll up from a short side, with the covering paper inside. Cool.

2 Unroll and remove the paper. Spread the sponge with buttercream or cream. Re-roll: make the first turn firmly, but roll more lightly after this turn. Put seam-side down on a wire rack and dust with icing sugar. Serve cut into slices.

Makes 8 Slices	EASY		NUTRITIONAL INFORMATION
	Preparation Time 25 minutes	**Cooking Time** 10–12 minutes, plus cooling	**Per Slice** 197 calories, 7.7g fat (of which 4g saturates), 29.2g carbohydrate, 0.1g salt

Cook's Tip

Chocolate Ganache: melt 200g (7oz) plain chocolate (at least 70% cocoa solids), broken into pieces, with 75g (3oz) butter in a heatproof bowl over a pan of gently simmering water, stirring occasionally. Stir the ganache until smooth.

Chocolate Marble Cake

175g (6oz) unsalted butter, softened
175g (6oz) golden caster sugar
3 medium eggs
125g (4oz) self-raising flour, sifted
50g (2oz) ground almonds
1 tsp baking powder, sifted
finely grated zest of 1 orange
1 tbsp brandy
4 tbsp cocoa powder, sifted
1 quantity chocolate ganache (see Cook's Tip)

For the decoration
50g (2oz) golden granulated sugar
juice of 1 orange
8 small kumquats

1 Preheat the oven to 190°C (170°C fan oven) mark 5. Line a 900g (2lb) loaf tin with baking parchment. Cream the butter with the caster sugar until pale and light. Beat in the eggs, one at a time. Fold the flour, almonds and baking powder into the bowl. Fold in the orange zest and brandy. Put half the mixture into a bowl and mix in the cocoa powder. Spoon alternate spoonfuls of both mixtures into the tin. Shake the tin once, then drag a skewer through the mixture. Bake for 45 minutes or until a skewer inserted into the centre comes out clean. Turn the cake out on to a wire rack and leave to cool. Peel off the lining paper, put the cake on the wire rack and position over a tray. Pour the chocolate ganache over the cake to cover it completely. Leave to set in a cool place for 30 minutes.

2 For the decoration, put the granulated sugar in a pan. Strain the orange juice into a jug, add enough water to make 150ml (¼ pint) and pour on to the sugar. Heat gently to dissolve. Add the kumquats and poach for 5–10 minutes; leave to cool. Arrange the kumquats on top of the cake. Cut into slices to serve.

EASY		NUTRITIONAL INFORMATION	Makes
Preparation Time 20 minutes	**Cooking Time** 45 minutes, plus cooling	**Per Slice** 617 calories, 40.2g fat (of which 23g saturates), 58.7g carbohydrate, 1g salt	**8** Slices

Chocolate Brandy Torte

125g (4oz) butter, diced, plus extra to grease

225g (8oz) plain chocolate (at least 70% cocoa solids), broken into pieces

3 large eggs, separated

125g (4oz) light muscovado sugar

50ml (2fl oz) brandy

75g (3oz) self-raising flour, sifted

50g (2oz) ground almonds

icing sugar, to dust

crème fraîche to serve

1 Preheat the oven to 180°C (160°C fan oven) mark 4. Grease and baseline a 20.5cm (8in) springform cake tin. Melt the diced butter and chocolate in a heatproof bowl over a pan of gently simmering water, stirring occasionally. Take the bowl off the pan and leave to cool a little.

2 Put the egg yolks and muscovado sugar in a bowl and whisk together until pale and creamy, then whisk in the brandy and melted chocolate on a slow speed. Fold in the flour and ground almonds with a large metal spoon. Put the mixture to one side.

3 Put the egg whites into a clean, grease-free bowl and whisk until they form soft peaks. Beat a large spoonful of the egg white into the chocolate mixture to lighten it, then carefully fold in the remainder with a large metal spoon.

4 Pour the mixture into the prepared tin and bake for 45 minutes or until a skewer inserted into the centre comes out clean. Leave the cake to cool in the tin for 10 minutes, then turn it out on to a wire rack. Remove the lining paper from the base of the cake when it's completely cold.

5 To serve, dust the top of the cake with sifted icing sugar and serve with crème fraîche.

Freezing Tip

Complete the recipe to the end of step 4, wrap, seal, label and freeze; it will keep for up to one month.
To use Thaw the torte at a cool room temperature for 2 hours. Dust with sifted icing sugar to serve.

Makes 6 Slices	EASY		NUTRITIONAL INFORMATION
	Preparation Time 10 minutes	**Cooking Time** 45 minutes, plus cooling	**Per Slice** 531 calories, 35g fat (of which 18.8g saturates), 46.7g carbohydrate, 0.5g salt

Get Ahead

Complete the recipe to the end of step 6. Wrap the cake in foil and store in an airtight container. It will keep for up to five days.
To use Complete the recipe.

Celebration Chocolate Cake

butter or sunflower oil to grease
200g (7oz) plain chocolate (at least 50% cocoa solids), broken into pieces
5 large eggs
125g (4oz) golden caster sugar
100g (3½oz) ground almonds
1 tbsp coffee liqueur, such as Tia Maria
fresh raspberries to decorate
icing sugar to dust

1 Grease a deep 12.5cm (5in) round cake tin and line with greaseproof paper, making sure the paper comes 5–7.5cm (2–3in) above the tin.

2 Melt the chocolate in a heatproof bowl over a pan of gently simmering water. Remove the bowl from the pan and leave to cool slightly. Meanwhile, preheat the oven to 170°C (150°C fan oven) mark 3.

3 Separate all but one of the eggs, putting the whites to one side. Whisk the yolks, the whole egg and the caster sugar at a high speed for 5 minutes or until the mixture is pale and leaves a ribbon trail when the whisk is lifted. Set the mixer to a very low speed, add the chocolate and then the almonds, and mix until evenly combined. Put to one side.

4 Put the egg whites into a clean, grease-free bowl and whisk until they form soft peaks. Beat one quarter of the egg whites into the chocolate mixture to loosen, then fold in the rest.

5 Pour the mixture into the prepared tin. Bake for 1–1¼ hours until a skewer inserted into the centre of the cake for 30 seconds comes out hot. Make several holes in the cake with the skewer, then pour the liqueur over it. Leave in the tin for 30 minutes, then turn out on to a wire rack and leave until cold.

6 Transfer to a plate, spoon raspberries on top and tie a ribbon around the cake. Dust with icing sugar.

Serves 16	EASY		NUTRITIONAL INFORMATION	
	Preparation Time 40 minutes	**Cooking Time** 1–1¼ hours, plus cooling	**Per Serving** 161 calories, 9g fat (of which 3g saturates), 17g carbohydrate, 0.1g salt	Gluten free • Dairy free

Cook's Tip

Store the Florentines in an airtight container; they will keep for up to two weeks.

Florentines

65g (2½oz) unsalted butter, plus extra to grease

50g (2oz) golden caster sugar

2 tbsp double cream

25g (1oz) sunflower seeds

20g (¾oz) chopped mixed candied peel

20g (¾oz) sultanas

25g (1oz) natural glacé cherries, roughly chopped

40g (1½oz) flaked almonds, lightly crushed

15g (½oz) plain flour

125g (4oz) plain chocolate (at least 70% cocoa solids), broken into pieces

1 Preheat the oven to 180°C (160°C fan oven) mark 4. Lightly grease two large baking sheets. Melt the butter in a small, heavy-based pan. Add the sugar and heat gently until dissolved, then bring to the boil. Take off the heat and stir in the cream, seeds, peel, sultanas, cherries, almonds and flour. Mix until evenly combined. Put heaped teaspoonfuls on to the baking sheets, spacing well apart to allow for spreading.

2 Bake one sheet at a time, for 6–8 minutes, until the biscuits have spread considerably and the edges are golden brown. Using a large, plain, metal biscuit cutter, push the edges into the centre to create neat rounds. Bake for a further 2 minutes or until deep golden. Leave on the baking sheet for 2 minutes, then transfer to a wire rack to cool completely.

3 Melt the chocolate in a heatproof bowl over a pan of gently simmering water, stirring occasionally. Spread on the underside of each Florentine and mark wavy lines with a fork. Put, chocolate side up, on a sheet of baking parchment until set.

EASY		NUTRITIONAL INFORMATION	Makes
Preparation Time 15 minutes	**Cooking Time** 8–10 minutes, plus cooling	**Per Biscuit** 115 calories, 7.8g fat (of which 3.8g saturates), 10.9g carbohydrate, 0.1g salt	**18**

Cook's Tips

Chocolate Ganache: melt 175g (6oz) plain chocolate (at least 70% cocoa solids), broken into pieces, in a heatproof bowl over a pan of simmering water. Add 75g (3oz) butter and 4 tbsp warmed double cream and stir everything together until smooth.

Store the cake in an airtight container. Eat within one week.

Sachertorte

175g (6oz) unsalted butter, at room temperature, plus extra to grease

175g (6oz) golden caster sugar

5 medium eggs, lightly beaten

3 tbsp cocoa powder

125g (4oz) self-raising flour

225g (8oz) plain chocolate (at least 70% cocoa solids), broken into pieces, melted (see page 10) and cooled for 5 minutes

4 tbsp brandy

1 quantity warm chocolate ganache (see Cook's Tips)

12 lilac sugar-coated almonds, or 50g (2oz) milk chocolate, melted

1 Preheat the oven to 190°C (170°C fan oven) mark 5. Grease and line a 20.5cm (8in) springform cake tin with baking parchment. Cream together the butter and sugar until pale and fluffy. Gradually beat in two-thirds of the beaten eggs – don't worry if the mixture curdles. Sift in the cocoa powder and 3 tbsp of the flour, then gradually beat in the remaining eggs. Fold in the remaining flour. Fold in the melted chocolate until evenly incorporated. Stir in 2 tbsp of the brandy. Put the mixture into the prepared tin and bake for 45 minutes. Cover the tin loosely with foil if browning too quickly. To test, insert a skewer into the centre of the cake; it should come out clean. Leave the cake to cool in the tin for 30 minutes.

2 Remove the cake from the tin, put on a wire rack and leave until cold. Drizzle with the remaining brandy. Position the wire rack over a tray. Ladle the ganache over the top of the cake, letting it trickle down the sides. Spread it evenly with a palette knife. Decorate with almonds, or melted chocolate. Allow to set.

Serves 12 Slices	A LITTLE EFFORT		NUTRITIONAL INFORMATION
	Preparation Time 35 minutes	**Cooking Time** 45–55 minutes, plus cooling	**Per Serving** 496 calories, 32.7g fat (of which 19.5g saturates), 45.3g carbohydrate, 0.7g salt

Chocolate and Chestnut Roulade

a little vegetable oil to grease

6 medium eggs, separated

200g (7oz) caster sugar, plus extra to dust

2–3 drops vanilla extract

50g (2oz) cocoa powder, sifted

For the filling

125g (4oz) plain chocolate (at least 50% cocoa solids), broken into pieces

300ml (½ pint) double cream

225g (8oz) unsweetened chestnut purée

200ml (7fl oz) full-fat crème fraîche

50g (2oz) icing sugar

1 Preheat the oven to 180°C (160°C fan oven) mark 4. Lightly oil a 33 x 20.5cm (13 x 8in) Swiss roll tin, then line it with greaseproof paper.

2 Put the egg yolks, caster sugar and vanilla into a large bowl. Whisk until pale and thick. Fold in the cocoa powder. Put the egg whites into a clean, grease-free bowl and whisk until they form stiff peaks. Fold into the cocoa mixture. Spoon into the tin and bake for 20–25 minutes until just cooked – the top should be springy to the touch. Leave to cool in the tin for 10–15 minutes. Dust a sheet of baking parchment with caster sugar. Carefully turn out the roulade on to the parchment. Leave to cool. Peel away the lining paper.

3 Melt the chocolate in a heatproof bowl over a pan of gently simmering water. In a separate bowl, lightly whip the cream. Beat the chestnut purée into the chocolate until smooth. Whisk in the crème fraîche and icing sugar. Beat 1 tbsp of the whipped cream into the chocolate mixture, then use a metal spoon to fold in half the remaining cream.

4 Spread the filling over the roulade, then spread the remaining cream on top. Roll up the roulade and lift on to a serving plate. Dust with caster sugar.

EASY		NUTRITIONAL INFORMATION		Serves
Preparation Time 20 minutes	**Cooking Time** 20–25 minutes, plus cooling	**Per Serving** 409 calories, 28g fat (of which 17g saturates), 36g carbohydrate, 0.3g salt	Gluten free	**10**

2

Cold Puddings

Get Ahead

Complete the recipe to the end of step 4 up to one day ahead. Cover and chill until needed.
To use Complete the recipe.

White Chocolate Mousse

100ml (3½fl oz) full-fat milk

1 cinnamon stick

250g (9oz) white chocolate, broken into pieces

300ml (½ pint) double cream

3 large egg whites

50g (2oz) plain chocolate

a little cocoa powder and ground cinnamon to decorate

1 Put the milk and cinnamon stick in a small pan and warm over a medium heat until the milk is almost boiling. Take the pan off the heat and set aside.

2 Melt the white chocolate in a heatproof bowl over a pan of gently simmering water. Take the bowl off the pan and leave to cool a little.

3 Strain the warm milk on to the melted chocolate and stir together until completely smooth. Leave to cool for 10 minutes.

4 Whip the cream until it just begins to hold its shape. Whisk the egg whites until soft peaks form. Fold the whipped cream into the chocolate mixture with a large metal spoon, then carefully fold in the egg whites. Spoon the mixture into six 150ml (¼ pint) bowls or glasses and chill for 4 hours or overnight.

5 Make curls using plain chocolate (see page 12). Sprinkle over the mousse. Dust with cocoa and a pinch of cinnamon.

	EASY		NUTRITIONAL INFORMATION	
Serves **6**	**Preparation Time** 15 minutes, plus minimum 4 hours chilling	**Cooking Time** 15 minutes, plus cooling	**Per Serving** 515 calories, 41g fat (of which 25g saturates), 31g carbohydrate, 0.2g salt	Gluten free

Chocolate Cinnamon Sorbet

200g (7oz) golden granulated sugar

50g (2oz) unsweetened cocoa powder

1 tsp instant espresso coffee powder

1 cinnamon stick

8 tsp crème de cacao (chocolate liqueur) to serve (optional)

1 Put the sugar into a large pan and add the cocoa powder, coffee and cinnamon stick with 600ml (1 pint) water. Bring to the boil, stirring until the sugar has completely dissolved. Boil for 5 minutes, then remove from the heat. Leave to cool. Discard the cinnamon stick, then chill.

2 If you have an ice-cream maker, put the mixture into it and churn for about 30 minutes until firm. (Alternatively, pour into a freezerproof container and put in the coldest part of the freezer until firmly frozen, then transfer the frozen mixture to a blender or food processor and blend until smooth. Quickly put the mixture back in the container and put it back into the freezer for at least 1 hour.)

3 To serve, scoop the sorbet into individual cups and, if you like, drizzle 1 tsp chocolate liqueur over each portion. Serve immediately.

EASY		NUTRITIONAL INFORMATION		Serves
Preparation Time 5 minutes, plus chilling and freezing	**Cooking Time** 15 minutes	**Per Serving** 118 calories, 1g fat (of which 1g saturates), 27g carbohydrate, 0.2g salt	Gluten Free • Dairy Free	**8**

Cheat's Chocolate Pots

500g carton fresh custard

200g (7oz) plain chocolate (at least 50 per cent cocoa solids), broken into pieces

1 Put the custard in a small pan with the chocolate pieces. Heat gently, stirring all the time, until the chocolate has melted.

2 Pour the mixture into four small coffee cups and chill in the fridge for 30 minutes to 1 hour before serving.

Try Something Different

Serve the mixture warm as a sauce for vanilla ice cream.

Serves	EASY		NUTRITIONAL INFORMATION
4	**Preparation Time** 5 minutes, plus chilling	**Cooking Time** 5 minutes	**Per Serving** 380 calories, 17g fat (of which 0g saturates), 53g carbohydrate, 0.0g salt [to come]

Cook's Tip

Vanilla Sauce: put 600ml (1 pint) double cream into a heavy-based pan. Scrape the seeds from a vanilla pod into the cream. Heat gently just to the boil, then leave to cool and infuse for about 15 minutes. Whisk 4 large egg yolks with 75g (3oz) golden caster sugar and ½ tsp cornflour in a bowl, add a little of the cooled cream and whisk until smooth. Add the remaining cream and stir well. Pour the sauce back into the rinsed-out pan and stir over a medium heat for 5 minutes or until thickened enough to lightly coat the back of the spoon. Strain, cool, cover and chill.

Rich Chocolate Terrine with Vanilla Sauce

oil to grease

350g (12oz) plain chocolate (at least 70% cocoa solids), broken into pieces

40g (1½oz) cocoa powder, plus extra to dust

6 large eggs, beaten

125g (4oz) light muscovado sugar

300ml (½ pint) double cream

5 tbsp brandy (optional)

1 quantity vanilla sauce to serve (see Cook's Tip)

1 Preheat the oven to 150°C (130°C fan oven) mark 2. Grease and baseline a 900g (2lb) loaf tin. Melt the chocolate with the cocoa powder in a heatproof bowl over a pan of simmering water, stirring occasionally. Take the bowl off the pan and leave to cool a little.

2 Whisk the eggs with the sugar until smooth and creamy. In another bowl, whip the cream until soft peaks form. Gradually fold the melted chocolate and cream into the egg mixture, then add the brandy, if you like. Pour into the tin and tap the tin to level the mixture. Stand the tin in a roasting tray. Fill the tray with hot water to come halfway up the sides. Cover with baking parchment. Bake in the oven for 1¾ hours or until the terrine is just set in the centre – it will firm up as it cools. Leave the tin in the tray of water for 30 minutes, then lift out, cool and chill overnight.

3 To serve, dip the loaf tin in a bowl of warm water for 10 seconds. Invert on to a board and shake to unmould. Cut into slices, using a warm, sharp knife. Dust with cocoa powder and serve with vanilla sauce.

Serves 12	A LITTLE EFFORT		NUTRITIONAL INFORMATION
	Preparation Time 45 minutes, plus overnight chilling	**Cooking Time** 1¾ hours, plus cooling	**Per Serving** 356 calories, 24.8g fat (of which 13.2g saturates), 33.6g carbohydrate, 0.2g salt

Cook's Tip

For a decorative top, use the tin to cut a circle of greaseproof paper, then fold to make eight triangles. Cut these out and put four on the cake and dust the uncovered cake with cocoa powder. Remove the triangles. Cover the cocoa with four triangles and dust the uncovered cake with icing sugar.

Italian Ice Cream Cake

400g (14oz) fresh cherries, pitted and quartered

4 tbsp amaretto liqueur

10 tbsp crème de cacao liqueur

200g (7oz) Savoiardi biscuits or sponge fingers

5 medium egg yolks

150g (5oz) golden caster sugar

450ml ($^3/_4$ pint) double cream, lightly whipped

1 tbsp vanilla extract

75g (3oz) pistachio nuts or hazelnuts, roughly chopped

75g (3oz) plain chocolate (at least 70% cocoa solids), roughly chopped

2–3 tbsp cocoa powder

2–3 tbsp golden icing sugar

1 Put the cherries and amaretto into a bowl, stir, cover with clingfilm and put to one side. Pour the crème de cacao into a shallow dish. Quickly dip a sponge finger into the liqueur on one side only, then cut in half lengthways to separate the sugary side from the base. Repeat with each biscuit.

2 Double-line a deep 24 x 4cm (9$^1/_2$ x 1$^1/_2$in) round tin with clingfilm. Arrange the sugar-coated sponge finger halves, sugar-side down, on the base of the tin. Drizzle with any remaining crème de cacao.

3 Put the yolks and caster sugar into a bowl and whisk until pale, light and fluffy. Fold in the cream, vanilla, nuts, chocolate and cherries with amaretto. Spoon on top of the sponge fingers in the tin and cover with the remaining sponge finger halves, cut-side down. Cover with clingfilm and freeze for at least 5 hours.

4 Upturn the cake on to a serving plate and remove the clingfilm. Sift cocoa powder and icing sugar over the cake and cut into wedges. Before serving, leave at room temperature for 20 minutes if the weather is warm, 40 minutes at cool room temperature, or 1 hour in the refrigerator, to allow the cherries to thaw and the ice cream to become mousse-like.

EASY	NUTRITIONAL INFORMATION	Serves
Preparation Time 30 minutes, plus 5 hours freezing and up to 1 hour softening	**Per Serving** 522 calories, 33g fat (of which 15g saturates), 46g carbohydrate, 0.2g salt	**10**

Mocha Ice Cream

600ml (1 pint) double cream
300ml (½ pint) semi-skimmed milk
6 large egg yolks
50g (2oz) golden caster sugar
150ml (¼ pint) strong espresso coffee, cooled
50g (2oz) plain chocolate chips

For the sauce

75g (3oz) plain chocolate (at least 70% cocoa solids),
broken into pieces
a few drops of vanilla extract

1 Put the cream and milk in a heavy-based pan and bring just to the boil. Meanwhile, whisk the egg yolks and sugar together in a bowl until pale and creamy. Slowly pour on the hot cream mixture, whisking all the time. Put back in the pan and heat gently, stirring with a wooden spoon until the custard thickens enough to lightly coat the back of the spoon.

2 Strain the custard into a bowl, stir in the coffee and set aside to cool. When cold, stir in the chocolate chips.

3 Pour into an ice-cream maker and churn for about 30 minutes, or according to the manufacturer's instructions, until frozen. (Alternatively, freeze the mixture in a freezerproof container, beating at hourly intervals to break down the ice crystals and ensure an even texture, until the ice cream is firmly frozen.)

4 About 30 minutes before serving, transfer the ice cream to the refrigerator to soften. Meanwhile, make the sauce. Put the chocolate, vanilla extract and 50ml (2fl oz) water into a pan and heat gently until the chocolate has melted. Bring to the boil and let it bubble for a few minutes until thickened; set aside to cool slightly.

5 Scoop the ice cream into serving bowls and pour the chocolate sauce over it. Serve at once.

	EASY		NUTRITIONAL INFORMATION
Serves 8	**Preparation Time** 20 minutes, plus freezing	**Cooking Time** 10–15 minutes, plus cooling	**Per Serving** 510 calories, 46g fat (of which 0g saturates), 21g carbohydrate, 0g salt

Chocolate Mousse

350g (12oz) plain chocolate (at least 70% cocoa solids), broken into pieces

6 tbsp rum, brandy or cold black coffee

6 large eggs, separated

a pinch of salt

chocolate curls, to decorate (see page 12)

1 Put the chocolate with the rum, brandy or black coffee in a heatproof bowl over a pan of gently simmering water. Leave to melt, stirring occasionally. Take the bowl off the pan and leave to cool slightly for 3–4 minutes, stirring frequently.

2 Beat the egg yolks with 2 tbsp water, then beat into the chocolate mixture until evenly blended.

3 Put the egg whites and salt into a clean, grease-free bowl and whisk until they form firm peaks, then fold into the chocolate mixture.

4 Pour the mixture into a 1.4–1.7 litre (2½–3 pint) soufflé dish or divide among eight 150ml (¼ pint) cups or ramekins. Chill for at least 4 hours, or overnight, until set. Decorate with chocolate curls.

EASY	NUTRITIONAL INFORMATION	Serves
Preparation Time 20 minutes, plus chilling	**Per Serving** 309 calories, 16.9g fat (of which 8.6g saturates), 28.4g carbohydrate, 0.1g salt	**8**

Chocolate Ice Cream

300ml (½ pint) semi-skimmed milk

1 vanilla pod, split

125g (4oz) plain chocolate (at least 70% cocoa solids), broken into pieces

3 large egg yolks

50–75g (2–3oz) golden caster sugar

300ml (½ pint) double cream

1 Pour the milk into a heavy-based pan, add the vanilla pod and chocolate, and heat gently until the chocolate has melted. Bring almost to the boil, then take off the heat and leave to infuse for 20 minutes.

2 Whisk the egg yolks and sugar together in a bowl until thick and creamy. Gradually whisk in the hot milk, then strain back into the pan. Cook over a low heat, stirring constantly with a wooden spoon, until the custard has thickened enough to lightly coat the back of the spoon; do not allow it to boil or it will curdle. Pour into a chilled bowl and allow to cool.

3 Add the double cream to the cold chocolate custard and whisk until evenly blended.

4 Pour into an ice-cream maker and churn for about 30 minutes or until frozen. (Alternatively, freeze in a shallow freezerproof container until firmly frozen, beating two or three times during freezing to break down the ice crystals and ensure an even texture.) Allow to soften at cool room temperature for 20–30 minutes before serving.

EASY		NUTRITIONAL INFORMATION	Serves
Preparation Time 20 minutes, plus infusing and freezing	**Cooking Time** 15 minutes	**Per Serving** 629 calories, 54.7g fat (of which 29.7g saturates), 38.9g carbohydrate, 0.2g salt	**4**

Boozy Panna Cotta

oil to grease
140ml (4½fl oz) double cream
150ml (¼ pint) semi-skimmed milk
3 tbsp light muscovado sugar
1 tbsp instant espresso coffee powder
50ml (2fl oz) Tia Maria or other coffee liqueur
40g (1½oz) plain chocolate (at least 70% cocoa solids), chopped
1½ tsp powdered gelatine
1 tsp vanilla extract
2 chocolate-coated coffee beans (optional)

1 Oil two 150ml (¼ pint) individual pudding basins and line them with clingfilm. Put 100ml (3½fl oz) cream into a small pan with the milk, sugar, coffee, 1 tbsp liqueur and the chocolate. Heat gently until the chocolate has melted, then bring to the boil.

2 Take off the heat, sprinkle the gelatine over the surface and leave for 5 minutes. Stir well to ensure the gelatine is fully dissolved, then add the vanilla extract and mix well. Strain the mixture through a sieve into a jug, then pour into the lined basins and chill for 2 hours.

3 To serve, unmould the panna cottas on to plates and remove the clingfilm. Stir the rest of the liqueur into the remaining cream and drizzle around the panna cottas. Top with chocolate-coated coffee beans, if you like.

Serves 2	EASY	NUTRITIONAL INFORMATION
	Preparation Time 20 minutes, plus chilling	**Per Serving** 622 calories, 44.7g fat (of which 25.2g saturates), 50.3g carbohydrate, 0.2g salt

Get Ahead

Bake the custards and allow to cool. Make the topping and cover the bowl. Cover the ramekins with clingfilm and chill, with the topping, for up to 24 hours.
To use Complete the recipe.

Baked Chocolate and Coffee Custards

300ml (½ pint) semi-skimmed milk

140ml (4½fl oz) double cream

200g (7oz) plain chocolate (at least 70% cocoa solids), broken into pieces

4 large egg yolks

1 tbsp golden caster sugar

3 tbsp very strong, cold black coffee

grated orange zest to decorate (optional)

thin shortbread biscuits to serve

For the topping

125g (4oz) mascarpone cheese

1 tsp icing sugar

grated zest and juice of ½ orange

1 Preheat the oven to 170°C (150°C fan oven) mark 3. Put the milk, cream and chocolate in a pan over a very gentle heat until melted. Stir until smooth.

2 Mix the egg yolks, sugar and coffee together in a bowl, then pour on the warm chocolate milk. Briefly mix, then strain through a sieve into a jug. Pour into six 150ml (¼ pint) ramekins, then stand them in a large roasting tin containing enough hot water to come halfway up their sides. Bake in the oven for 20–25 minutes until just set and still a little wobbly in the middle – they will firm as they cool. Lift the dishes out of the roasting tin and leave to cool, then stand on a small tray and chill for at least 3 hours.

3 To make the topping, beat the mascarpone, icing sugar, orange zest and juice together until smooth. Cover and chill for 1–2 hours. To serve, put a spoonful of the mascarpone mixture on top of each custard and decorate with grated orange zest, if you like. Serve with thin shortbread biscuits.

EASY		NUTRITIONAL INFORMATION	Serves
Preparation Time 15 minutes, plus chilling	**Cooking Time** 20–25 minutes, plus cooling	**Per Serving** 448 calories, 36.7g fat (of which 20.4g saturates), 28.2g carbohydrate, 0.3g salt	**6**

Cook's Tips

To line the soufflé dish, cut a double strip of greaseproof paper long enough to go around the soufflé dish with the ends overlapping slightly, and deep enough to reach from the bottom of the dish to about 7cm (2³/₄in) above the rim. Wrap the paper around the dish and secure under the rim with string or an elastic band, so that it fits closely to the top of the dish.

Once the soufflé has set, remove the string or elastic band and ease the paper away with a knife dipped in hot water. Whip the remaining cream until thick and pipe it around the top edge of the soufflé. Top with chocolate curls or grated chocolate and serve.

Cold Chocolate Soufflé

3 large eggs, separated

75g (3oz) golden caster sugar

75g (3oz) plain chocolate (at least 70% cocoa solids), broken into pieces

1 tbsp powdered gelatine

1 tbsp brandy

300ml (½ pint) double cream

chocolate curls (see page 12), or coarsely grated chocolate

1 Prepare a 600ml (1 pint) soufflé dish, 12.5cm (5in) in diameter (see Cook's Tips). Whisk the egg yolks and sugar together in a heatproof bowl over a pan of hot water, until thick and creamy. Remove from the heat and whisk from time to time until cool. Melt the chocolate in a heatproof bowl over a pan of gently simmering water, then leave to cool a little.

2 Put 2 tbsp water into a small bowl, sprinkle on the gelatine and leave to soften for 10 minutes. Stand this bowl over a pan of simmering water until the gelatine has dissolved. Cool slightly, then pour it into the egg mixture in a steady stream, stirring. Stir the melted chocolate and the brandy into the egg mixture. Leave to cool until it is almost at the point of setting.

3 Lightly whip half the cream and fold it into the chocolate mixture. Put the egg whites into a clean, grease-free bowl and whisk until stiff but not dry. Lightly fold them into the mixture. Pour into the prepared soufflé dish and chill for 2–3 hours until set. To decorate, see Cook's Tips.

Serves 4	EASY	NUTRITIONAL INFORMATION
	Preparation Time 20 minutes, plus chilling	**Per Serving** 585 calories, 49.9g fat (of which 26.8g saturates), 33.8g carbohydrate, 0.2

Rich Chocolate Pots

300g (11oz) plain chocolate (at least 70% cocoa solids),
broken into pieces

300ml (½ pint) double cream

250g (9oz) mascarpone cheese

3 tbsp cognac

1 tbsp vanilla extract

6 tbsp crème fraîche

chocolate curls to decorate (see page 12)

1 Melt the plain chocolate in a heatproof bowl over a pan of gently simmering water. Remove from the heat and add the cream, mascarpone, cognac and vanilla. Mix well – the hot chocolate will melt into the cream and mascarpone.

2 Divide the mixture among six 150ml (¼ pint) glasses, and chill for 20 minutes. Spoon some crème fraîche on top of each chocolate pot, and decorate with the chocolate curls.

EASY		NUTRITIONAL INFORMATION		Serves
Preparation Time 10 minutes, plus 20 minutes chilling	**Cooking Time** 10 minutes	**Per Serving** 895 calories, 66g fat (of which 41g saturates), 66g carbohydrate, 0g salt	Gluten free	**6**

Tiramisù

250ml (9fl oz) cold coffee

2 tbsp coffee liqueur, such as Kahlúa or Tia Maria

24 Savoiardi biscuits or sponge fingers

2 medium eggs, separated

3 tbsp icing sugar

500g (1lb 2oz) quark

1 tsp vanilla extract

cocoa powder to dust

1 Pour the cold coffee and coffee liqueur into a bowl. Dip 12 of the sponge fingers into the liquid, and put into six serving dishes or one large dish.

2 Put the egg whites into a clean, grease-free bowl and whisk until they form soft peaks. In a separate bowl, whisk together the egg yolks, icing sugar, quark and vanilla. Fold in the egg whites.

3 Spoon half the quark mixture over the sponges. Dip the remaining sponge fingers in the coffee mixture, then put on top. Cover with the remaining quark mixture. Liberally dust with cocoa powder and serve.

Cook's Tip

Quark is a smooth, soft white cheese, with a texture between yogurt and fromage frais. Fromage frais can be used instead.

Serves 6	EASY	NUTRITIONAL INFORMATION
	Preparation Time 20 minutes	**Per Serving** 344 calories, 16g fat (of which 4g saturates), 39g carbohydrate, 0.5g salt

Baked Ricotta Torte

125g (4oz) digestive biscuits

50g (2oz) butter, melted

75g (3oz) dark muscovado sugar

250g (9oz) ricotta cheese

grated zest of 1 lemon, plus 3 tbsp juice

300ml (½ pint) natural yogurt

25g (1oz) rice flour, or ground rice

3 large eggs

cocoa powder to dust

chocolate curls to decorate (see page 12)

1 Line the base of a 23cm (9in) springform cake tin with baking parchment. Crush the biscuits to a fine powder in a food processor. (Alternatively, put them in a plastic bag and crush with a rolling pin.) Pour the butter into the biscuits in the processor and pulse until the mixture comes together. (Or tip the crushed biscuits into a bowl and stir in the melted butter.) Press over the base of the tin and chill for about 30 minutes.

2 Preheat the oven to 180°C (160°C fan oven) mark 4. Put the sugar in the processor and whiz for 1–2 minutes. Add the ricotta and process for 2–3 minutes, then add the lemon zest and juice, yogurt and rice flour or ground rice. Pulse to mix well, then add the eggs and combine. (Alternatively, put the sugar in a bowl and use an electric hand mixer to blend in the ricotta, then the lemon zest, juice, yogurt and flour. Briefly mix in the eggs.)

3 Pour the ricotta mixture over the biscuit base and bake for 40 minutes or until lightly set. Leave to cool in the tin, then chill until ready to serve.

4 Unmould the torte and liberally dust with cocoa powder. Top with chocolate curls to finish.

Serves 8	EASY		NUTRITIONAL INFORMATION
	Preparation Time 20 minutes, plus chilling	**Cooking Time** 40 minutes, plus cooling	**Per Serving** 354 calories, 25.6g fat (of which 14.8g saturates), 25.8g carbohydrate, 0.7g salt

Chocolate Meringue Roulade

5 large egg whites

175g (6oz) golden caster sugar

1 tsp cornflour

125g (4oz) chocolate spread

4 tbsp half-fat crème fraîche

50g (2oz) cooked vacuum-packed chestnuts, roughly chopped (optional)

icing sugar and cocoa powder to dust

1 Preheat the oven to 110°C (90°C fan oven) mark ¼. Line a 30.5 x 21cm (12 x 8½in) Swiss roll tin with baking parchment. Whisk the eggs whites in a large bowl until frothy, then whisk in the sugar. Stand the bowl over a pan of gently simmering water and whisk for 4–5 minutes at high speed until very thick and shiny. Off the heat, whisk in the cornflour. Spoon into the tin and level. Bake for 1 hour or until just firm on top. Leave to cool for 1 hour; don't worry if the meringue weeps.

2 Put the chocolate spread in a bowl and beat in the crème fraîche. Fold in the chopped chestnuts, if using.

3 Turn the meringue out on to a sheet of baking parchment dusted with icing sugar and carefully peel off the lining parchment. Make a shallow cut in the meringue, 2.5cm (1in) in from the edge of a short end. Spread the chocolate mixture over the meringue and roll it up, from the cut end. Dust with icing sugar and cocoa powder.

EASY		NUTRITIONAL INFORMATION	Serves
Preparation Time 30 minutes	**Cooking Time** 1 hour, plus cooling	**Per Serving** 279 calories, 9.6g fat (of which 1.1g saturates), 47.4g carbohydrate, 0.1g salt	**6**

Freezing Tip

Complete the recipe to the end of step 4, then cool, wrap, seal, label and freeze.

To use Put the frozen buns on a baking sheet in the oven at 220°C (200°C fan oven) mark 7 for 5 minutes. Cool, then complete the recipe.

Profiteroles

65g (2½oz) plain flour
a pinch of salt
50g (2oz) butter, diced
2 large eggs, lightly beaten
300ml (½ pint) double cream
a few drops of vanilla extract
1 tsp caster sugar

For the chocolate sauce

225g (8oz) plain chocolate (at least 70% cocoa solids), broken into pieces
140ml (4½fl oz) double cream
1–2 tbsp Grand Marnier to taste (optional)
1–2 tsp golden caster sugar to taste (optional)

1 Preheat the oven to 220°C (200°C fan oven) mark 7. Sift the flour with the salt on to a sheet of greaseproof paper. Put the butter into a medium heavy-based pan with 150ml (¼ pint) water. Heat gently until the butter melts, then bring to a rapid boil. Take off the heat and immediately tip in all the flour and beat thoroughly with a wooden spoon until the mixture is smooth and forms a ball. Turn into a bowl and leave to cool for about 10 minutes.

2 Gradually add the eggs to the mixture, beating well after each addition. Ensure that the mixture becomes thick and shiny before adding any more egg – if it's added too quickly, the choux paste will become runny and the cooked buns will be flat.

3 Sprinkle a large baking sheet with a little water. Using two damp teaspoons, spoon about 18 small mounds of the choux paste on to the baking sheet, spacing well apart to allow room for them to expand. (Alternatively, spoon the choux paste into a piping bag fitted with a 1cm (½in) plain nozzle and pipe mounds on to the baking sheet.)

4 Bake for about 25 minutes or until well risen, crisp and golden brown. Make a small hole in the side of each bun to allow the steam to escape and then put back in the oven for a further 5 minutes or until thoroughly dried out. Slide on to a large wire rack and set aside to cool.

5 To make the sauce, put the chocolate and cream in a medium pan with 4 tbsp water. Heat gently, stirring occasionally, until the chocolate melts to a smooth sauce; do not boil. Remove from the heat.

6 To assemble, lightly whip the cream with the vanilla extract and sugar until it just holds its shape. Pipe into the hole in each choux bun, or split the buns open and spoon in the cream. Chill for up to 2 hours.

7 Just before serving, gently reheat the chocolate sauce. Add Grand Marnier and sugar to taste, if you like. Divide the choux buns among serving bowls and pour over the warm chocolate sauce. Serve immediately.

A LITTLE EFFORT		NUTRITIONAL INFORMATION	Serves
Preparation Time 25 minutes	**Cooking Time** 30 minutes, plus cooling	**Per Serving** 652 calories, 59.1g fat (of which 33.4g saturates), 35.4g carbohydrate, 0.3g salt	**6**

3

Fruit and Nut

Raspberry and White Chocolate Tarts

225g (8oz) plain flour, plus extra to dust

150g (5oz) butter, cut into cubes

50g (2oz) icing sugar, plus extra to dust

2–3 drops of vanilla extract

1 large egg, lightly beaten

350–450g (12oz–1lb) raspberries

pouring cream to serve

For the filling

275g (10oz) good-quality white chocolate, broken into small pieces

300ml (½ pint) double cream

1 vanilla pod, split

2 large eggs, separated

2 tbsp Kirsch

1 Put the flour, butter and icing sugar into a food processor and pulse until the mixture resembles fine crumbs. (Alternatively, rub the butter into the flour and sugar in a large bowl by hand or using a pastry cutter.) Add the vanilla extract and all but 2 tsp of the beaten egg. Pulse, or stir with a fork, until the dough comes together to form a ball. Wrap in clingfilm and chill for at least 30 minutes.

2 Roll out the pastry thinly on a lightly floured surface. Cut out rounds and use to line eight 9cm (3½in),

3cm (1¼in) deep, loose-based tart tins. If the pastry cracks as you line the tins, just patch together. Prick the pastry with a fork, then chill for 30 minutes. Preheat the oven to 200°C (180°C fan oven) mark 6.

3 Line the pastry cases with greaseproof paper and baking beans and bake 'blind' for 10 minutes. Remove the paper and beans and bake for 5–10 minutes to cook the bases. Brush with the reserved egg and bake for 1 minute longer to seal; cool slightly. Reduce the oven temperature to 190°C (170°C fan oven) mark 5.

4 To make the filling, put the chocolate in a bowl. Pour the cream into a small, heavy-based pan, add the vanilla and bring just to the boil. Take off the heat and remove the vanilla. Slowly pour the cream on to the chocolate and stir until the chocolate is melted. Cool. Mix the egg yolks and Kirsch into the cooled chocolate mixture. Put the egg whites into a clean, grease-free bowl and whisk until they form soft peaks, then fold carefully into the chocolate mixture until evenly incorporated. Pour the filling into the pastry cases and bake for 10–15 minutes until just set. If the filling appears to colour too quickly in the oven, cover with foil. Leave to cool in the tins. Don't worry if the filling seems very soft – it will become firmer on chilling. Chill for at least 5 hours or overnight.

5 Remove from the refrigerator 30 minutes before serving. Unmould on to plates. Arrange the raspberries on top. Dust with icing sugar and serve with cream.

Serves 8	A LITTLE EFFORT		NUTRITIONAL INFORMATION
	Preparation Time 40 minutes, plus chilling	**Cooking Time** 40 minutes	**Per Serving** 648 calories, 48.7g fat (of which 28.3g saturates), 51.5g carbohydrate, 0.6g salt

Hot Pear and White Chocolate Puddings

100g (3½oz) butter, softened, plus extra to grease
100g (3½oz) self-raising flour, sifted
100g (3½oz) light muscovado sugar
1 tsp cocoa powder
1 medium egg
2–3 drops of almond extract
50g (2oz) white chocolate, chopped
2 ripe pears
25g (1oz) flaked almonds

1 Preheat the oven to 180°C (160°C fan oven) mark 4. Lightly grease four 250ml (9fl oz) ramekins.

2 Put half the butter, half the flour and half the muscovado sugar in a bowl. Add the cocoa powder, egg and almond extract, and beat together until smooth. Divide the mixture among the prepared ramekins. Scatter half the chocolate on top.

3 Peel, core and chop the pears, then divide among the ramekins.

4 In a bowl, rub together the remaining butter, flour and sugar until the mixture resembles breadcrumbs. Stir in the flaked almonds and the remaining chocolate, then sprinkle over the pears and bake for 20 minutes or until golden. Serve hot.

Serves	EASY		NUTRITIONAL INFORMATION
4	**Preparation Time** 20 minutes	**Cooking Time** 20 minutes	**Per Serving** 524 calories, 30g fat (of which 16g saturates), 61g carbohydrate, 0.5g salt

Cook's Tip

Remember to remove the carton of custard from the refrigerator 20 minutes before you start to make the trifle, to bring it to room temperature.

3 x 500g bags frozen mixed berries

125g (4oz) golden caster sugar, plus 1 tsp

250g (9oz) biscotti or cantuccini biscuits

5 tbsp dessert wine or fruit juice (such as cranberry and orange)

White Chocolate and Red Fruit Trifle

For the topping

450ml (¾ pint) double cream, lightly whipped

200g (7oz) good-quality white chocolate, broken into pieces and melted (see page 10)

500g carton fresh custard (at room temperature)

500ml (18fl oz) crème fraîche, beaten until smooth

1 Put the berries into a large pan with 125g (4oz) caster sugar, and heat gently for about 5 minutes or until the sugar has dissolved and the berries have thawed. Sieve the mixture over a bowl to catch the juices. Pour the juices back into the pan, then tip the berries into the bowl. Bring the juices to the boil and simmer for 10 minutes or until reduced to about 150ml (¼ pint). Pour over the berries and leave to cool. Lay the biscuits over the base of a 3 litre (5¼ pint) trifle dish and sprinkle with the dessert wine or fruit juice. Scatter the cooled berries over the top.

2 Transfer half the cream to a bowl, cover and chill; leave the rest at room temperature. Pour the melted chocolate into a cold bowl and gradually fold in the custard. Fold in the room-temperature whipped cream. Pour the chocolate custard over the fruit to cover it evenly. Fold the chilled cream into the crème fraîche with the 1 tsp sugar, then spoon over the custard. Chill for 2 hours. Remove from refrigerator 20 minutes before serving.

EASY		NUTRITIONAL INFORMATION	Serves
Preparation Time 45 minutes, plus chilling	**Cooking Time** 15 minutes	**Per Serving** 943 calories, 68.3g fat (of which 40.6g saturates), 81.6g carbohydrate, 0.5g salt	**8**

150g (5oz) plain chocolate (at least 70% cocoa solids), chopped or grated

100g (3½oz) plain flour

1 large egg

a pinch of salt

300ml (½ pint) semi-skimmed milk

25g (1oz) butter

1 tbsp light muscovado sugar

4 bananas, thickly sliced

125ml (4fl oz) brandy

sunflower oil for frying

icing sugar to dust

Chocolate and Banana Crêpes

1   Set half the chocolate to one side and put the remainder in a food processor or blender with the flour, egg, salt and milk. Whiz until smooth. Pour the batter into a jug, cover and chill for 30 minutes.

2   Melt the butter and sugar in a frying pan. Add the bananas and stir-fry over medium heat for 3 minutes. Carefully add the brandy. Simmer for 2 minutes until the bananas soften and the liquid is syrupy; set aside.

3   Brush an 18cm (7in) non-stick crêpe pan or small frying pan with oil and heat up. Stir the batter, then pour about 4 tbsp into the pan to thinly coat the base. Cook for 2 minutes or until golden brown. Cook the other side for 1 minute. Transfer to a plate and keep warm. Repeat with the remaining batter.

4   Put two spoonfuls of banana filling on one half of each crêpe and scatter the reserved chocolate on top. Fold in half, then in half again; keep warm while filling the remaining crêpes. Dust with icing sugar and serve.

Serves 4	EASY		NUTRITIONAL INFORMATION
	Preparation Time 15 minutes, plus chilling	**Cooking Time** 30–40 minutes	**Per Serving** 656 calories, 30.3g fat (of which 12.3g saturates), 74.6g carbohydrate, 0.3g salt

Try Something Different

Turn this into a fun chocolate fondue by offering different fruits for dunking, such as mango, pineapple chunks and raspberries, or even marshmallows. Provide a pile of cocktail sticks for spearing the fruit.

Chocolate-dipped Strawberries

100g (3¹/₂oz) milk chocolate, broken into pieces

100g (3¹/₂oz) white chocolate, broken into pieces

100g (3¹/₂oz) plain chocolate (at least 70% cocoa solids), broken into pieces

700g (1¹/₂lb) strawberries

1 Put each type of chocolate side by side in a single heatproof serving bowl, keeping each type as separate as you can.

2 Melt the chocolate over a pan of gently simmering water, then, holding each strawberry by its stalk, dip it into the chocolate. Arrange the strawberries in a shallow bowl to serve. Alternatively, let everyone dunk the berries themselves.

EASY		NUTRITIONAL INFORMATION		Serves
Preparation Time 10 minutes	**Cooking Time** About 10 minutes	**Per Serving** 291 calories, 15g fat (of which 9g saturates), 37g carbohydrate, 0.1g salt	Gluten free	**6**

Orange and Chocolate Cheesecake

225g (8oz) chilled butter, plus extra to grease

250g (9oz) plain flour, sifted

150g (5oz) light muscovado sugar

3 tbsp cocoa powder

chocolate curls to decorate (see page 12) (optional)

For the topping

2 oranges

800g (1lb 12oz) full-fat cream cheese

250g (9oz) mascarpone cheese

4 large eggs

225g (8oz) golden caster sugar

2 tbsp cornflour

1/2 tsp vanilla extract

1 vanilla pod

1 Preheat the oven to 180°C (160°C fan oven) mark 4. Grease and baseline a 23cm (9in) springform cake tin. Cut 175g (6oz) of the butter into cubes. Melt the remaining butter and set aside. Put the flour and cubed butter into a food processor with the sugar and cocoa powder. Whiz together until the texture of fine breadcrumbs. (Alternatively, rub the butter into the flour in a large bowl by hand or using a pastry cutter. Stir in the sugar and cocoa.) Pour in the melted butter and pulse, or stir with a fork, until the mixture comes together.

2 Spoon into the prepared tin and press with the back of a metal spoon to level the surface. Bake for 35–40 minutes until lightly puffed; avoid over-browning, or the biscuit base will have a bitter flavour. Remove from the oven and allow to cool. Reduce the oven temperature to 150°C (130°C fan oven) mark 2.

3 Meanwhile, make the topping. Grate the zest from the oranges, then squeeze the juice – you will need 150ml (1/4 pint). Put the cream cheese, mascarpone, eggs, sugar, cornflour, grated orange zest and vanilla extract into a large bowl. Using an electric whisk, beat the ingredients together thoroughly until well combined.

4 Split the vanilla pod in half lengthways, scrape out the seeds, using the tip of a sharp knife, and add them to the cheese mixture. Beat in the orange juice and continue whisking until the mixture is smooth.

5 Pour the cheese mixture over the cooled biscuit base. Bake for about 1 1/2 hours or until pale golden on top, slightly risen and just set around the edge. The cheesecake should still be slightly wobbly in the middle; it will set as it cools. Turn off the oven and leave the cheesecake inside to cool for 1 hour. Remove and allow to cool completely (about 3 hours).

6 Just before serving, unclip the tin and transfer the cheesecake to a plate. Scatter chocolate curls on top to decorate, if you like.

EASY		NUTRITIONAL INFORMATION	Serves
Preparation Time 45 minutes	**Cooking Time** 2–2 1/4 hours, plus cooling	**Per Serving** 767 calories, 59.8g fat (of which 37.2g saturates), 53.1g carbohydrate, 1.2g salt	**12**

Freezing Tip

Complete the recipe up to the end of step 4. Once the muffins are cold, pack, seal, label and freeze for up to one month.
To use Thaw at a cool room temperature or individually in the microwave, allowing 30 seconds on full power.

Chocolate Banana Muffins

275g (10oz) self-raising flour
1 tsp bicarbonate of soda
½ tsp salt
3 large bananas, about 450g (1lb)
125g (4oz) golden caster sugar
1 large egg, beaten
50ml (2fl oz) semi-skimmed milk
75g (3oz) unsalted butter, melted and cooled
50g (2oz) plain chocolate, chopped

1 Preheat the oven to 180°C (160°C fan oven) mark 4. Line a bun tin or muffin pan with 12 paper muffin cases. Sift the flour, bicarbonate of soda and salt together into a large mixing bowl and put to one side.

2 Peel the bananas and mash with a fork in a bowl. Add the sugar, egg, milk and melted butter, and mix until well combined.

3 Add this to the flour mixture, with the chopped chocolate. Stir gently, using only a few strokes, until the flour is only just incorporated – do not over-mix. The mixture should be lumpy.

4 Spoon the mixture into the muffin cases, half-filling them. Bake in the oven for 20 minutes or until the muffins are well risen and golden. Transfer to a wire rack to cool. Serve warm or cold.

Makes 12	EASY		NUTRITIONAL INFORMATION
	Preparation Time 15 minutes	**Cooking Time** 20 minutes, plus cooling	**Per Muffin** 228 calories, 7g fat (of which 4g saturates), 40g carbohydrate, 0.5g salt

Try Something Different

Tropical Fruit and Coconut Flapjacks: replace the hazelnuts and chocolate with chopped, dried mixed tropical fruit. Replace 50g (2oz) of the oats with desiccated coconut.

Apricot and Mixed Seed Flapjacks: replace the hazelnuts with 50g (2oz) mixed seeds (such as pumpkin, sunflower, linseed and sesame). Reduce the oats to 125g (4oz) and replace the chocolate with 100g (3½oz) chopped dried apricots.

Hazelnut and Chocolate Flapjacks

125g (4oz) unsalted butter, plus extra to grease

125g (4oz) light muscovado sugar

1 tbsp golden syrup

50g (2oz) hazelnuts, roughly chopped

175g (6oz) jumbo or porridge oats

50g (2oz) plain chocolate, roughly chopped

1 Preheat the oven to 180°C (160°C fan oven) mark 4. Lightly grease a shallow 28 x 18cm (11 x 7in) baking tin.

2 Put the butter, sugar and golden syrup in a pan and melt together over a low heat. Stir in the hazelnuts and oats. Leave the mixture to cool slightly, then stir in the chocolate.

3 Spoon the mixture into the prepared tin and bake for about 30 minutes or until golden and firm.

4 Leave to cool in the tin for a few minutes, then cut into 12 pieces. Turn out on to a wire rack and leave to cool completely. Store in an airtight container for up to one week.

EASY		NUTRITIONAL INFORMATION	Makes
Preparation Time 10 minutes	**Cooking Time** 30 minutes, plus cooling	**Per Flapjack** 229 calories, 14g fat (of which 6g saturates), 26g carbohydrate, 0.2g salt	**12**

White Chocolate and Nut Brownies

75g (3oz) unsalted butter, plus extra to grease

500g (1lb 2oz) white chocolate, roughly chopped

3 large eggs

175g (6oz) golden caster sugar

175g (6oz) self-raising flour

a pinch of salt

175g (6oz) macadamia nuts, roughly chopped

1 tsp vanilla extract

1 Preheat the oven to 190°C (170°C fan oven) mark 5. Grease and line a 25.5 x 20.5cm (10 x 8in) baking tin.

2 Melt 125g (4oz) white chocolate with the butter in a heatproof bowl over a pan of gently simmering water, stirring occasionally. Remove the bowl from the pan and leave to cool slightly.

3 Whisk the eggs and sugar together in a large bowl until smooth, then gradually beat in the melted chocolate mixture; the consistency will become quite firm. Sift the flour and salt over the mixture, then fold in with the nuts, the remaining chopped chocolate and the vanilla extract.

4 Turn the mixture into the prepared tin and level the surface. Bake for 30–35 minutes until risen and golden and the centre is just firm to the touch – the mixture will still be soft under the crust; it firms up on cooling. Leave to cool in the tin. Turn out and cut into 12 squares. Store in an airtight container; they will keep for up to one week.

Makes 12	EASY		NUTRITIONAL INFORMATION
	Preparation Time 20 minutes	**Cooking Time** 30–35 minutes, plus cooling	**Per Brownie** 502 calories, 31g fat (of which 13g saturates), 52g carbohydrate, 0.4g salt

Freezing Tip

Complete the recipe to step 4. Wrap, seal, label and freeze for up to one month.
To use Thaw overnight at a cool room temperature. Complete the recipe.

Chocolate and Cherry Gateau

350g (12oz) fresh cherries, pitted (see page 27), or 400g can pitted cherries, drained, plus extra cherries to serve

3 tbsp dark rum

125g (4oz) butter, softened, plus extra to grease

350g (12oz) plain chocolate (at least 70% cocoa solids), broken into pieces

3 large eggs, separated

125g (4oz) caster sugar

50g (2oz) ground almonds

50g (2oz) plain flour, sifted

450ml (¾ pint) double cream

chocolate curls (see page 12) and cocoa powder

1 Put the cherries in a bowl with 2 tbsp rum. Cover and soak for at least 6 hours.

2 Preheat the oven to 180°C (160°C fan oven) mark 4. Grease a deep 23cm (9in) round cake tin and line the base with greaseproof paper. Melt 150g (5oz)

chocolate with 3 tbsp water in a heatproof bowl over a pan of simmering water. Remove from the heat, add the remaining rum and the egg yolks and beat until smooth. Put the butter and sugar in a bowl and beat until pale and fluffy. Stir in the chocolate mixture. Fold in the flour and almonds. Whisk the egg whites until soft peaks form, then fold into the chocolate mixture. Pour into the tin and bake for 30–35 minutes until a skewer comes out clean with a few crumbs on it. Cool in the tin for 10 minutes, then turn out on to a wire rack until cold.

3 Put the remaining chocolate into a bowl. Bring the cream to the boil, pour over the chocolate and leave for 5 minutes. Stir until the chocolate has melted. Cool, then beat the mixture until thick and pale. Clean the cake tin, put the cake back in it and spoon the cherries and any juice over the top. Spread the chocolate cream on top and smooth the surface, then cover and chill for at least 2 hours. Decorate with chocolate curls, dust with cocoa and serve the cake with fresh cherries.

EASY		NUTRITIONAL INFORMATION	Serves
Preparation Time 1 hour, plus 8 hours soaking and chilling	**Cooking Time** 45 minutes, plus cooling	**Per Serving** 537 calories, 41g fat (of which 23g saturates), 38g carbohydrate, 0.2g salt	**12**

Chocolate and Cherry Amaretti Tart

400g (14oz) pitted bottled or canned morello cherries, drained

3 tbsp brandy, sloe gin or almond-flavoured liqueur

150g (5oz) butter, softened

50g (2oz) icing sugar, plus extra to dust

1 small egg, beaten

225g (8oz) plain flour, plus extra to dust

For the filling

100g (3½oz) plain chocolate, broken into pieces

125g (4oz) butter, softened

125g (4oz) caster sugar

3 large eggs, beaten

125g (4oz) ground almonds

25g (1oz) self-raising flour, sifted

50g (2oz) amaretti biscuits, crushed

75g (3oz) slivered or flaked almonds

1 Put the cherries in a bowl with the brandy, gin or liqueur and leave for 30 minutes or overnight. Put the butter, icing sugar and egg in a food processor and whiz until almost smooth. Add the flour and whiz until the mixture begins to form a dough. (Alternatively, rub the fat into the flour by hand or using a pastry cutter to resemble fine crumbs, then stir in the icing sugar and egg.) Knead the pastry lightly, then wrap and chill for 30 minutes.

2 Roll out the pastry on a lightly floured worksurface and line a 23cm (9in) loose-based fluted tart tin. Chill for 20 minutes. Preheat the oven to 200°C (180°C fan oven) mark 6. Line the pastry base with greaseproof paper and baking beans, and bake for 15 minutes. Remove the paper and beans and put back in the oven for 5 minutes. Reduce the oven temperature to 150°C (130°C fan oven) mark 2.

3 To make the filling, melt the chocolate in a heatproof bowl over a pan of gently simmering water. Stir once or twice until smooth. Cool. In a bowl, beat the butter with the sugar until pale and fluffy. Gradually beat in the eggs, alternating with the almonds and flour. Fold in the melted chocolate and biscuits. Spoon one-third of the mixture over the base of the pastry case. Spoon the cherries and juice over. Spread the remaining filling over the cherries. Sprinkle on the almonds and bake for about 1 hour. The tart will have a thin top crust but will be soft underneath. Leave in the tin for 10–15 minutes to firm up, then unmould, dust with icing sugar and serve warm.

Freezing Tip

Complete the recipe but do not dust with icing sugar. Cool completely, wrap, seal, label and freeze for up to one month.
To use Thaw at a cool room temperature overnight. Warm through at 200°C (180°C fan oven) mark 6 for 10 minutes and dust with icing sugar before serving.

Serves 8	EASY		NUTRITIONAL INFORMATION
	Preparation Time 30 minutes, plus chilling	**Cooking Time** 1½ hours, plus 10–15 minutes cooling	**Per Serving** 760 calories, 50g fat (of which 22g saturates), 67g carbohydrate, 0.8g salt

Luxury Chocolate Orange Torte

75g (3oz) butter, diced, plus extra to grease

100g (3½oz) plain chocolate (at least 70% cocoa solids), broken into pieces

6 medium eggs

225g (8oz) golden caster sugar

150g (5oz) ground almonds, sifted

grated zest and juice of 1 orange

strawberries and raspberries to serve

1 Preheat the oven to 190°C (170°C fan oven) mark 5. Grease a 20.5cm (8in) springform cake tin and line with greaseproof paper.

2 Melt the butter and chocolate in a heatproof bowl set over a pan of gently simmering water, stirring occasionally. Remove the bowl from the pan and set aside to cool a little.

3 Put the eggs and sugar into a large bowl and mix with an electric whisk until the volume has tripled and the mixture is thick and foamy – it will take about 5–10 minutes. Add the ground almonds, orange zest and juice to the egg mixture, then gently fold together with a metal spoon.

4 Pour about two-thirds of the mixture into the prepared tin. Add the melted chocolate and butter to the remaining mixture and fold together. Add to the tin and swirl around just once or twice to create a marbled effect. Bake in the oven for 50 minutes– 1 hour. Leave to cool in the tin, then carefully remove and slice. Serve with strawberries and raspberries.

Serves	A LITTLE EFFORT		NUTRITIONAL INFORMATION	
12	**Preparation Time** 30 minutes	**Cooking Time** 55 minutes–1 hour 5 minutes, plus cooling	**Per Serving** 231 calories, 12g fat (of which 3g saturates), 25g carbohydrate, 0.1g salt	Gluten free

4 large eggs, separated

125g (4oz) golden caster sugar, plus extra to dust

125g (4oz) plain chocolate (at least 70% cocoa solids), broken into pieces, melted (see page 10) and cooled a little

cocoa powder and icing sugar to dust

For the filling

140ml (4½fl oz) whipping cream

1 tsp icing sugar

75ml (2½fl oz) Greek yogurt

2 x 425g cans morello cherries, drained, pitted and halved

Black Forest Roulade

1 Preheat the oven to 180°C (160°C fan oven) mark 4. Line a 33 x 23cm (13 x 9in) Swiss roll tin with baking parchment.

2 Whisk the egg yolks with the sugar in a large bowl until thick and creamy. Whisk in the melted chocolate. Whisk the egg whites in a clean, grease-free bowl until they form stiff peaks. Fold into the chocolate mixture. Pour into the tin, level the surface and bake for 20 minutes or until firm to the touch.

3 Turn the roulade out on to a sugar-dusted sheet of greaseproof paper and peel off the lining parchment. Cover with a damp cloth and leave to cool for 30 minutes.

4 To make the filling, lightly whip the cream with the icing sugar, then fold in the yogurt. Spread over the cold roulade and scatter the cherries on top. Roll up from one of the narrow ends, using the greaseproof paper to help. Chill for 30 minutes. Slice the roulade and serve, dusted with cocoa powder and icing sugar.

EASY		NUTRITIONAL INFORMATION	Serves
Preparation Time 35 minutes	**Cooking Time** 20 minutes, plus cooling	**Per Serving** 248 calories, 12.1g fat (of which 6.6g saturates), 33.1g carbohydrate, 0.1g salt	**10**

Cook's Tip

To make the caramel, dissolve 125g (4oz) caster sugar in a small, heavy-based pan over a low heat. Bring to the boil and bubble until a golden caramel colour. Dip each physalis into the caramel, then put on an oiled baking sheet and leave to cool.

Get Ahead

Complete the recipe up to the end of step 3, then store the meringues in an airtight container; they will keep for up to one week.
To use Complete the recipe.

Chocolate and Hazelnut Meringues

125g (4oz) hazelnuts, toasted and skinned

125g (4oz) caster sugar

75g (3oz) plain chocolate (at least 70% cocoa solids), broken into pieces

2 medium egg whites

300ml (½ pint) double cream

redcurrants, blackberries and chocolate shavings to decorate

physalis (Cape gooseberries) dipped in caramel (see Cook's Tip), to serve

1 Preheat the oven to 110°C (90°C fan oven) mark ¼. Line two baking sheets with baking parchment. Put the nuts in a food processor with 3 tbsp of the sugar and whiz to a fine powder. (Alternatively, chop the nuts by hand as finely as possible and add all the sugar at step 2.) Add the chocolate and pulse until roughly chopped, or chop by hand. Whisk the egg whites in a clean, grease-free bowl until stiff. Whisk in the remaining sugar a spoonful at a time until the mixture is stiff and shiny. Fold in the nut mixture.

2 Spoon the mixture in small, rough mounds on to the baking sheets and bake for about 45 minutes or until the meringues will just peel off the paper. Push in the base of each meringue to form a hollow. Cook for 1¼ hours or until crisp and dry. Leave to cool.

3 Whip the cream lightly. Spoon three-quarters into the meringues. Chill for up to 2 hours, then decorate with the remaining cream, fruit and chocolate shavings. Serve immediately with caramelised physalis.

Serves	A LITTLE EFFORT		NUTRITIONAL INFORMATION	
6	**Preparation Time** 25 minutes, plus 2 hours softening	**Cooking Time** 2 hours, plus cooling	**Per Serving** 520 calories, 42g fat (of which 19g saturates), 32g carbohydrate, 0.1g salt	Gluten free

Try Something Different

Use raspberries instead of strawberries, leaving them whole.
Try lightly toasted flaked almonds instead of the hazelnuts.

Strawberries with Chocolate Meringue

225g (8oz) strawberries, chopped
finely grated zest of ½ orange
125g (4oz) caster sugar, plus 1 tbsp extra
3 large egg whites
1 tbsp cocoa powder, sifted
15g (½oz) hazelnuts, toasted and chopped

1 Preheat the oven to 150°C (130°C fan oven) mark 2. Mix together the strawberries, orange zest and 1 tbsp caster sugar. Divide among six ramekins.

2 Put the egg whites into a clean, grease-free bowl and whisk until they form soft peaks. Add the remaining sugar and whisk until the whites are stiff and shiny. Fold in the cocoa powder.

3 Spoon this chocolate meringue over the fruit and sprinkle the hazelnuts on top.

4 Bake in the oven for 20–25 minutes until the meringue is crisp on the outside and soft in the middle. Serve immediately.

EASY		NUTRITIONAL INFORMATION		Serves
Preparation Time 15 minutes	**Cooking Time** 20–25 minutes	**Per Serving** 132 calories, 2g fat (of which trace saturates), 27g carbohydrate, 0.1g salt	Gluten free • Dairy free	**6**

4

Warm Puddings

Quick Gooey Chocolate Puddings

100g (3¹/₂oz) butter, plus extra to grease

100g (3¹/₂oz) golden caster sugar, plus extra to dust

100g (3¹/₂oz) plain chocolate (at least 70% cocoa solids), broken into pieces

2 large eggs

20g (³/₄oz) plain flour

icing sugar to dust

1 Preheat the oven to 200°C (180°C fan oven) mark 6. Butter four 200ml (7fl oz) ramekins and dust with sugar. Melt the chocolate and butter in a heatproof bowl over a pan of gently simmering water. Take the bowl off the pan and leave to cool for 5 minutes.

2 Whisk the eggs, caster sugar and flour together in a bowl until smooth. Fold in the chocolate mixture and pour into the ramekins.

3 Stand the dishes on a baking tray and bake for 12–15 minutes until the puddings are puffed and set on the outside, but still runny inside. Turn out, dust with icing sugar and serve immediately.

Serves 4	EASY		NUTRITIONAL INFORMATION
	Preparation Time 15 minutes	**Cooking Time** 12–15 minutes	**Per Serving** 468 calories, 30.6g fat (of which 18.5g saturates), 46.2g carbohydrate, 0.6g salt

Try Something Different

Replace the brandy with Grand Marnier and use orange-flavoured plain chocolate.

Chocolate Crêpes with a Boozy Sauce

100g (3½oz) plain flour, sifted

a pinch of salt

1 medium egg

300ml (½ pint) semi-skimmed milk

sunflower oil for frying

50g (2oz) plain chocolate (at least 70% cocoa solids), roughly chopped

100g (3½oz) unsalted butter

100g (3½oz) light muscovado sugar, plus extra to sprinkle

4 tbsp brandy

1 Put the flour and salt in a bowl, make a well in the centre and add the egg. Use a balloon whisk to mix the egg with a little of the flour, then gradually add the milk to make a smooth batter. Cover and leave to stand for about 20 minutes.

2 Pour the batter into a jug. Heat 1 tsp oil in a 23cm (9in) frying pan, then pour in 100ml (3½fl oz) batter, tilting the pan so that the mixture coats the bottom, and fry for 1–2 minutes until golden underneath. Turn carefully and fry the other side. Tip on to a plate, cover with greaseproof paper and repeat with the remaining batter, using more oil as needed.

3 Divide the chocolate among the crêpes. Fold each crêpe in half, and then in half again.

4 Put the butter and sugar in a heavy-based frying pan over a low heat. Add the brandy and stir. Slide the crêpes into the pan and cook for 3–4 minutes to melt the chocolate. Serve drizzled with sauce and sprinkled with sugar.

Serves 4	EASY		NUTRITIONAL INFORMATION
	Preparation Time 5 minutes, plus standing	**Cooking Time** 10–15 minutes	**Per Serving** 594 calories, 35g fat (of which 17g saturates), 57g carbohydrate, 0.5g salt

Cook's Tip

Lay a greased and pleated sheet of foil or a double thickness of greaseproof paper over the top of the bowl and secure under the rim with string.

75g (3oz) butter, plus extra to grease

75g (3oz) golden caster sugar

50g (2oz) plain chocolate (at least 60% cocoa solids), broken into pieces, melted (see page 10) and cooled for 5 minutes

1 medium egg, separated

1/2–1 tsp vanilla extract

125g (4oz) breadcrumbs

50g (2oz) self-raising flour, sifted

4–5 tbsp semi-skimmed milk

Chocolate Crumb Pudding

For the chocolate fudge sauce

50g (2oz) unsalted butter

50g (2oz) light muscovado sugar

50g (2oz) plain chocolate (at least 70% cocoa solids), broken into pieces

100ml (3 1/2 fl oz) double cream

1 Half-fill a steamer or large pan with water and put it on to boil. Grease a 900ml (1 1/2 pint) pudding basin. Cream the butter with the sugar in a bowl until pale and fluffy. Beat in the chocolate, egg yolk and vanilla. Combine the breadcrumbs and flour. Fold half into the mixture with 2 tbsp milk, then fold in the rest with enough milk to give a soft, dropping consistency. Whisk the egg white in a clean, grease-free bowl until it forms soft peaks. Fold into the mixture, then spoon into the basin and cover (see Cook's Tip). Lower into the pan, cover tightly and steam for 1 1/4–1 1/2 hours. Top up the pan with boiling water as necessary.

2 To make the sauce, put the butter, sugar and chocolate in a small, heavy-based pan and heat gently until the chocolate is melted. Pour in the cream, slowly bring to the boil and let it bubble for 3 minutes or until the sauce is glossy and thickened. Allow the sauce to cool slightly. Lift the basin out of the pan and remove the foil or greaseproof paper. Turn out the pudding on to a warmed plate. Serve with the hot chocolate fudge sauce.

A LITTLE EFFORT		NUTRITIONAL INFORMATION	Serves
Preparation Time 20 minutes	**Cooking Time** 1 1/4–1 1/2 hours	**Per Serving** 776 calories, 48.7g fat (of which 29.2g saturates), 84.2g carbohydrate, 1.4g salt	**4**

Chocolate Panettone Pudding

125g (4oz) raisins

100ml (3½fl oz) brandy

75g (3oz) softened butter, plus extra to grease

700g (1½lb) panettone

2 x 500g cartons fresh custard, or 750ml (1¼ pints) home-made

600ml (1 pint) semi-skimmed milk

200g (7oz) plain chocolate (at least 70% cocoa solids), roughly chopped

icing sugar to dust

1 Put the raisins in a bowl, pour on the brandy, cover and leave to soak overnight.

2 Preheat the oven to 180°C (160°C fan oven) mark 4. Grease a 3.4 litre (6 pint) ovenproof dish. Slice the panettone into slices about 5mm (¼in) thick. Spread with the butter and cut into quarters. Stir the custard and milk together and pour a thin layer over the base of the prepared dish. Arrange a layer of panettone on top and scatter some of the raisins and chocolate. Pour on another thin layer of custard. Continue to layer up the panettone, raisins, chocolate and custard, finishing with a layer of custard. Leave to rest for 1 hour.

3 Stand the dish in a roasting tin and pour hot water around the dish to come halfway up the sides. Bake in the oven for 1–1¼ hours or until the custard is set and the top has turned a deep brown, covering lightly with foil after 40 minutes to prevent over-browning. Dust the surface lightly with icing sugar to serve.

Serves 8	A LITTLE EFFORT		NUTRITIONAL INFORMATION
	Preparation Time 30 minutes, plus overnight soaking and 1 hour standing	**Cooking Time** 1–1¼ hours	**Per Serving** 685 calories, 25.1g fat (of which 10g saturates), 97.3g carbohydrate, 0.9g salt

Double Chocolate Baked Alaskas

50g (2oz) melted butter, plus extra to grease
200g (7oz) plain chocolate digestive biscuits
600ml (1 pint) good-quality chocolate ice cream
2 chocolate flake bars, roughly chopped
4 large egg whites
(225g) 8oz golden caster sugar
50g (2oz) desiccated coconut
cocoa powder, to dust
toasted coconut shavings (optional)

1 Lightly grease a baking sheet. Crush the biscuits to a fine powder in a food processor. (Alternatively, put them in a plastic bag and crush with a rolling pin, then transfer to a bowl.) Stir in the hot, melted butter. Using a 6.5cm (2½in) pastry cutter as a template, press the mixture into six rounds on the baking sheet and freeze for 30 minutes.

2 Beat the ice cream to soften it slightly and pile it into mounds on the biscuit bases. Make a shallow hollow in the centre of each ice cream mound and fill with the chopped chocolate flakes. Put back in the freezer for at least 1 hour or until firm.

3 Put the egg whites and sugar in a large bowl set over a pan of barely simmering water. Using an electric whisk, beat for 10 minutes or until the mixture is thick and glossy. Fold in the desiccated coconut. Allow to cool for 5 minutes.

4 Cover the ice cream mounds completely with a thick layer of meringue. Put back in the freezer for at least 4 hours or overnight.

5 To serve, preheat the oven to 220°C (200°C fan oven) mark 7, then bake the puddings for 5 minutes or until golden. Dust with cocoa powder, top with toasted coconut, if you like, and serve immediately.

A LITTLE EFFORT		NUTRITIONAL INFORMATION	Serves
Preparation Time 20 minutes, plus freezing	**Cooking Time** 5 minutes	**Per Serving** 630 calories, 30g fat (of which 0g saturates), 84g carbohydrate, 0g salt	**6**

Chocolate and Prune Pudding

600ml (1 pint) skimmed milk

50g (2oz) plain chocolate (at least 70% cocoa solids), broken into pieces, or chocolate chips

2 large eggs

2 large egg yolks

40g (1½oz) light brown sugar

½ tsp cornflour

2 tbsp unsweetened cocoa powder, plus extra to dust

100g (3½oz) ready-to-eat prunes, chopped

1 Preheat the oven to 170°C (150°C fan oven) mark 3. Heat the milk to simmering point, then remove from the heat. Add the broken chocolate and stir until it has melted completely.

2 Whisk together the eggs, egg yolks, sugar, cornflour and cocoa powder in a heatproof bowl until smooth. Gradually pour in the hot chocolate milk, stirring until it is combined.

3 Put the prunes into the base of individual ovenproof dishes, or serving dish, then strain in the milk mixture through a sieve. Put the dishes in a roasting tin and fill the tin with boiling water so that it comes halfway up the sides of the dishes. Bake in the oven for 30–40 minutes until just set.

4 Remove the dishes from the roasting tin and serve warm. Alternatively, leave to cool, then chill until ready to serve. Dust with cocoa powder before serving.

EASY		NUTRITIONAL INFORMATION		Serves
Preparation Time 10 minutes	**Cooking Time** 30–40 minutes	**Per Serving** 195 calories, 8g fat (of which 4g saturates), 24g carbohydrate, 0.3g salt	Gluten free	**6**

Mocha Soufflés

50g (2oz) plain chocolate (at least 70% cocoa solids),
roughly chopped

1 tbsp cornflour

1 tbsp cocoa powder

1–1½ tsp instant coffee granules

4 tbsp golden caster sugar

150ml (¼ pint) skimmed milk

2 egg yolks

3 egg whites

icing sugar or cocoa powder to dust

1 Preheat the oven to 190°C (170°C fan oven) mark 5 and put a baking sheet inside to heat up. Put the chocolate in a non-stick pan with the cornflour, cocoa powder, coffee granules, 1 tbsp caster sugar and the milk. Warm gently, stirring over a low heat, until the chocolate has melted. Increase the heat and cook, stirring continuously, until the mixture just thickens. Leave to cool a little, then stir in the egg yolks. Cover the surface with a piece of damp greaseproof paper and allow to cool.

2 Put the egg whites into a clean, grease-free bowl and whisk until they form soft peaks. Gradually whisk in the remaining caster sugar, a spoonful at a time, until the meringue is stiff but not dry.

3 Stir a third of the meringue into the cooled chocolate mixture to lighten it, then gently fold in the remainder, using a large metal spoon. Divide the mixture among six 150ml (¼ pint) ramekins or ovenproof tea or coffee cups. Stand them on the hot baking sheet and bake for about 12 minutes or until puffed up.

4 Dust the soufflés with icing sugar or cocoa powder and serve immediately.

Serves 6	EASY		NUTRITIONAL INFORMATION
	Preparation Time 15 minutes	Cooking Time 12 minutes	Per Serving 132 calories, 4.9g fat (of which 2.3g saturates), 19.7g carbohydrate, 0.2g salt

Try Something Different

Instead of baguette, use croissants or brioche for a richer pudding.

Chocolate Bread Pudding

200g (7oz) baguette

100g (3½oz) milk chocolate, roughly chopped

500g carton fresh custard

150ml (¼ pint) semi-skimmed milk

1 large egg, beaten

butter to grease

1 tbsp demerara sugar

50g (2oz) walnuts, finely chopped

50g (2oz) plain or milk chocolate, in chunks

single cream to serve (optional)

1 Roughly chop the baguette and put it into a large bowl. Put the chopped milk chocolate in a pan with the custard and milk over a low heat. Stir gently until the chocolate has melted. Beat in the egg.

2 Pour the chocolate mixture over the bread, stir well to coat, then cover and chill for at least 4 hours.

3 Preheat the oven to 180°C (160°C fan oven) mark 4. Spoon the soaked bread into a buttered 1.4 litre (2½ pint), 7.5cm (3in) deep ovenproof dish, then bake for 30–40 minutes.

4 Sprinkle with the sugar, walnuts and chocolate chunks. Put the dish back in the oven for 20–30 minutes until lightly set. Serve the pudding warm, with single cream if you like.

A LITTLE EFFORT		NUTRITIONAL INFORMATION	Serves
Preparation Time 20 minutes, plus minimum 4 hours chilling	**Cooking Time** 55 minutes–1¼ hours	**Per Serving** 390 calories, 17g fat (of which 6g saturates), 51g carbohydrate, 0.7g salt	**6**

Dark Chocolate Soufflés

50g (2oz) plain chocolate (at least 70% cocoa solids), broken into pieces

2 tbsp cornflour

1 tbsp cocoa powder

1 tsp instant coffee granules

4 tbsp golden caster sugar

150ml (¼ pint) skimmed milk

2 medium eggs, separated, plus 1 egg white

1 Preheat the oven to 190°C (170°C fan oven) mark 5, and put a baking sheet inside to heat up. Put the chocolate in a pan with the cornflour, cocoa powder, coffee, 1 tbsp caster sugar and the milk. Warm gently to melt the chocolate. Increase the heat and stir until the mixture thickens. Allow to cool a little, then stir in the egg yolks. Cover with damp greaseproof paper.

2 Whisk the egg whites in a clean, grease-free bowl until soft peaks form. Gradually whisk in the remaining caster sugar until the mixture is stiff.

3 Stir one-third of the egg whites into the chocolate mixture. Fold in the remaining whites and divide among six 150ml (¼ pint) ramekins. Put the ramekins on a baking sheet and bake for 12 minutes or until well risen. Serve immediately.

Try Something Different

Use flavoured plain chocolate for an unusual twist, such as ginger, mint or even chilli.

Serves	EASY		NUTRITIONAL INFORMATION	
6	**Preparation Time** 20 minutes	**Cooking Time** 20 minutes	**Per Serving** 134 calories, 4g fat (of which 2g saturates), 22g carbohydrate, 0.1g salt	Gluten free

Cook's Tip

Chocolate custard: put 4 tbsp custard powder and 4 tsp sugar in a heatproof bowl. Add enough of 450ml ($^3/_4$ pint) skimmed milk to make a smooth paste. Heat the remaining milk until almost boiling, then stir into the custard paste. Put the mixture back in the pan. Add 40g (1$^1/_2$oz) white chocolate drops and stir until the chocolate has melted and the custard has thickened.

Chocolate Puddings with Chocolate Custard

25g (1oz) hazelnuts

125g (4oz) butter, plus extra to grease

75g (3oz) light muscovado sugar

75g (3oz) self-raising flour

$^1/_2$ tsp baking powder

2 tbsp cocoa powder, plus extra to dust

25g (1oz) plain chocolate (at least 70% cocoa solids), roughly chopped

2 large eggs, beaten

chocolate custard to serve (see Cook's Tip)

1 Preheat the oven to 180°C (160°C fan oven) mark 4. Grease six 150ml ($^1/_4$ pint) ramekins and line the bases with baking parchment.

2 Spread the hazelnuts over a baking sheet. Toast under a hot grill until light golden brown, turning them frequently. Put the hazelnuts in a clean teatowel and rub off the skins. Roughly chop the nuts. Put the butter and sugar in a pan and heat gently until combined. Cool.

3 Sift the flour, baking powder and cocoa powder into a bowl. Stir in the nuts and chocolate. Make a well in the centre; pour in the butter mixture and eggs, and beat well. Pour the mixture into the prepared ramekins and bake for 20–25 minutes until just firm to the touch. Cool slightly and turn out; keep warm.

4 Trim the top from each pudding and put upside down on six serving plates. Dust with cocoa powder, pour the chocolate custard around them and serve.

Serves	EASY		NUTRITIONAL INFORMATION
6	**Preparation Time** 20 minutes	**Cooking Time** 20–25 minutes	**Per Serving** Per Serving 333 calories, 24g fat (of which 13.3g saturates), 26g carbohydrate, 0.7g salt

Warm Chocolate Fondants

butter to grease

3 medium eggs, plus 3 egg yolks

50g (2oz) golden caster sugar

175g (6oz) plain chocolate (at least 70% cocoa solids), broken into pieces

150g (5oz) unsalted butter

50g (2oz) plain flour, sifted

6 chocolate truffles

1 Preheat the oven to 200°C (180°C fan oven) mark 6. Lightly grease six 200ml (7fl oz) ramekins. Put the eggs, egg yolks and sugar in a large bowl and beat with an electric whisk for 8–10 minutes until pale and fluffy.

2 Meanwhile, melt the chocolate and butter in a heatproof bowl set over a pan of gently simmering water, stirring occasionally.

3 Stir a spoonful of the melted chocolate into the egg mixture, then gently fold the remaining chocolate mixture into the egg mixture.

4 Put a large spoonful of mixture into each ramekin. Put a chocolate truffle in the centre of each, taking care not to push it down. Divide the remainder of the mixture among the ramekins to cover the truffle; they should be about three-quarters full. Bake for 10–12 minutes until the top is firm and starting to rise and crack. Serve warm.

EASY		NUTRITIONAL INFORMATION	Serves
Preparation Time 25 minutes	**Cooking Time** 10–12 minutes	**Per Serving** 502 calories, 37g fat (of which 21g saturates), 39g carbohydrate, 0.5g salt	**6**

Banana and Chocolate Bread Pudding

225g (8oz) crustless white bread

butter to grease

2 bananas

4 medium eggs

175g (6oz) golden caster sugar

300ml (½ pint) double cream

300ml (½ pint) semi-skimmed milk

2 tsp vanilla extract

½ tsp ground cinnamon

150g (5oz) plain chocolate (at least 70% cocoa solids), roughly chopped

50g (2oz) shelled pecan nuts, roughly chopped

pouring cream or vanilla ice cream to serve

1 Cut the bread into bite-size cubes and spread out on a board. Leave to dry out for at least 4 hours.

2 Preheat the oven to 190°C (170°C fan oven) mark 5. Butter a shallow 2 litre (3½ pint) ovenproof dish. Peel the bananas and mash in a bowl using a fork, then beat in the eggs. Stir in the sugar, cream, milk, vanilla extract and cinnamon. Fold the chocolate and pecan nuts into the mixture with the bread cubes, then pour into the prepared dish.

3 Bake the pudding in the oven for 50 minutes or until the top is firm and golden brown. Leave to stand for about 10 minutes to allow the custard to firm up slightly. Spoon into warmed serving bowls and serve with cream or vanilla ice cream.

Get Ahead

Bake the pudding up to one day ahead, allow to cool, then cover and chill.

To use Reheat the pudding in the oven at 190°C (170°C fan oven) mark 5 for about 15 minutes.

EASY		NUTRITIONAL INFORMATION	Serves
Preparation Time 15 minutes, plus 4 hours drying	**Cooking Time** 50 minutes, plus 10 minutes standing	**Per Serving** 720 calories, 45.4g fat (of which 21.4g saturates), 77.2g carbohydrate, 0.7g salt	**6**

Chocolate Steamed Sponge Pudding

125g (4oz) butter, plus extra to grease

4 tbsp cocoa powder

125g (4oz) golden caster sugar

a few drops of vanilla extract

2 large eggs, beaten

175g (6oz) self-raising flour, sifted

2–4 tbsp semi-skimmed milk

custard to serve

1 Half-fill a steamer or large pan with water and put on to boil. Grease a 900ml (1½ pint) pudding basin. Blend the cocoa powder with 2 tbsp hot water to a smooth cream; allow to cool. Cream the butter and sugar together in a bowl until pale and fluffy. Stir in the vanilla extract, then the cooled blended cocoa.

2 Add the eggs, a little at a time, beating well after each addition. Using a metal spoon, fold in half the sifted flour, then fold in the remainder, with enough milk to give a dropping consistency.

3 Spoon the mixture into the basin. Lay a greased and pleated sheet of foil or a double thickness of greaseproof paper over the top of the bowl and secure under the rim with string. Lower into the pan, cover tightly and steam for 1½ hours, topping up the pan with boiling water as necessary.

4 Lift out the basin and remove the foil or greaseproof paper. Turn out the pudding on to a warmed plate and serve with custard.

Serves 4	EASY		NUTRITIONAL INFORMATION
	Preparation Time 20 minutes	**Cooking Time** 1½ hours	**Per Serving** 584 calories, 32.1g fat (of which 19.7g saturates), 67.8g carbohydrate, 1.4g salt

Cook's Tip

Freeze leftover egg yolks with a pinch of salt for savoury use, or a pinch of sugar if you plan to add them to sweet recipes.

Gooey Chocolate Soufflés

125g (4oz) golden caster sugar

50g (2oz) cocoa powder

9 egg whites, at room temperature

a pinch of cream of tartar

15g (½oz) plain chocolate (at least 70% cocoa solids), coarsely grated or finely chopped

2 tsp dark rum

1 tsp vanilla extract

1 Preheat the oven to 180°C (160°C fan oven) mark 4. Sift 100g (3½oz) caster sugar together with the cocoa powder. Put to one side.

2 Put the egg whites and cream of tartar into a clean, grease-free bowl and whisk until foamy. Continue whisking at high speed, gradually adding the remaining sugar a spoonful at a time, until the mixture holds stiff peaks.

3 Using a large metal spoon, carefully fold the sugar and cocoa mixture into the meringue with the chocolate, rum and vanilla extract. The mixture should be evenly combined but still stiff.

4 Divide the mixture among eight 175ml (6fl oz) ovenproof tea or coffee cups, or ramekins. Stand the cups in a large roasting tin and pour enough boiling water into the tin to come at least halfway up their sides. Bake for 12–15 minutes until puffed and set around the edges but still soft in the centre. Serve.

EASY		NUTRITIONAL INFORMATION	Serves
Preparation Time 10 minutes	**Cooking Time** 12–15 minutes	**Per Serving** 106 calories, 1.9g fat (of which 1.1g saturates), 18.2g carbohydrate, 0.3g salt	**8**

5

Biscuits and Treats

Chocolate Fudge Shortbread

175g (6oz) butter, at room temperature, diced, plus extra to grease
250g (9oz) plain flour
75g (3oz) golden caster sugar

For the topping

2 x 397g cans sweetened condensed milk
100g (3½oz) light muscovado sugar
100g (3½oz) butter
250g (9oz) plain chocolate (at least 70% cocoa solids), broken into pieces

1 Preheat the oven to 180°C (160°C fan oven) mark 4. Grease and line a 33 x 23cm (13 x 9in) Swiss roll tin with baking parchment. Put the flour, caster sugar and butter in a food processor and blend until the mixture forms crumbs, then pulse a little more until it forms a ball. (Alternatively, use a food mixer.) Turn out on to a lightly floured surface and knead lightly to combine.

2 Press the mixture into the prepared tin and bake for 20 minutes or until firm to the touch and very pale brown.

3 To make the topping, put the condensed milk, sugar and butter into a non-stick pan and cook over a medium heat, stirring continuously. (Alternatively, put into a large bowl and microwave on full power for 12 minutes or until the mixture is thick and fudgey, beating with a balloon whisk every 2–3 minutes.) Spoon the caramel on to the shortbread, smooth over and allow to cool.

4 To finish, melt the chocolate in a heatproof bowl over a pan of gently simmering water, then pour over the caramel layer. Leave to set at room temperature, then cut into squares to serve.

Makes 20 Squares	EASY		NUTRITIONAL INFORMATION
	Preparation Time 30 minutes	**Cooking Time** 20 minutes, plus cooling	**Per Square** 369 calories, 18.8g fat (of which 11.9g saturates), 47.8g carbohydrate, 0.4g salt

Try Something Different

Cranberry, Hazelnut and Orange Biscotti: increase the flour to 375g (13oz), omit the cocoa powder and add the grated zest of 1 orange. Replace the chocolate chips with dried cranberries and the pistachio nuts with chopped blanched hazelnuts.

Chocolate and Pistachio Biscotti

300g (11oz) plain flour, sifted
75g (3oz) cocoa powder, sifted
1 tsp baking powder
150g (5oz) plain chocolate chips
150g (5oz) shelled pistachio nuts
a pinch of salt
75g (3oz) unsalted butter, softened
225g (8oz) granulated sugar
2 large eggs, beaten
1 tbsp icing sugar

1 Preheat the oven to 180°C (160°C fan oven) mark 4 and line a large baking sheet with baking parchment. In a large bowl, mix together the flour, cocoa powder, baking powder, chocolate chips, pistachio nuts and salt.

2 Put the butter and granulated sugar into a large bowl. Using an electric whisk, beat together until light and fluffy. Gradually whisk in the eggs.

3 Stir the dry ingredients into the mixture until it forms a stiff dough. With floured hands, shape the dough into two slightly flattened logs, each about 30.5 x 5cm (12 x 2in). Sprinkle with icing sugar. Put the logs on to the prepared baking sheet and bake for 40–45 minutes until they are slightly firm to the touch.

4 Leave the logs on the baking sheet for 10 minutes, then cut diagonally into slices 2cm (³/₄in) thick. Arrange them, cut-side down, on the baking sheet and bake again for 15 minutes or until crisp. Cool on a wire rack.

Makes 30	EASY		NUTRITIONAL INFORMATION
	Preparation Time 15 minutes	**Cooking Time** about 1 hour, plus cooling	**Per Biscuit** 152 calories, 7g fat (of which 3g saturates), 20g carbohydrate, 0.2g salt

White and Dark Chocolate Cookies

125g (4oz) unsalted butter, softened, plus extra to grease

125g (4oz) golden caster sugar

2 medium eggs, beaten

2 tsp vanilla extract

250g (9oz) self-raising flour, sifted

finely grated zest of 1 orange

100g (3½oz) white chocolate, roughly chopped

100g (3½oz) plain chocolate (at least 70% cocoa solids), roughly chopped

1 Cream together the butter and sugar until the mixture is pale and fluffy. Gradually beat in the eggs and vanilla extract. Sift in the flour, add the orange zest, then add the white and plain chocolate. Mix the dough together with your hands. Knead lightly, then wrap in clingfilm. Chill the cookie mixture for at least 30 minutes.

2 Preheat the oven to 180°C (160°C fan oven) mark 4 and grease three baking sheets.

3 Divide the mixture into 26 pieces and roll each into a ball. Flatten each ball slightly to make a disc, then put on to the prepared baking sheets, spaced well apart. Bake for 10–12 minutes until golden.

4 Leave on the baking sheet for 5 minutes, then transfer to a wire rack to cool completely.

EASY		NUTRITIONAL INFORMATION	Makes
Preparation Time 15 minutes, plus 30 minutes chilling	**Cooking Time** 10–12 minutes, plus cooling	**Per Cookie** 133 calories, 7g fat (of which 4g saturates), 17g carbohydrate, 0.1g salt	**26**

Chilled Chocolate Biscuit Cake

125g (4oz) unsalted butter, chopped, plus extra to grease

150g (5oz) plain chocolate, broken into pieces

250g (9oz) panforte, chopped

100g (3½oz) Rich Tea biscuits, chopped

2–3 tbsp Amaretto, rum or brandy

ice cream to serve (optional)

1 Grease an 18cm (7in) square cake tin and baseline with baking parchment. Melt the butter and chocolate in a heatproof bowl over a pan of gently simmering water, stirring occasionally. Take the bowl off the pan and leave to cool a little.

2 In a large bowl, mix the panforte, biscuits and Amaretto, rum or brandy. Add the melted chocolate mixture and stir to coat.

3 Pour the mixture into the cake tin and chill for at least 2 hours. Cut into wedges and serve with ice cream, if you like.

EASY		NUTRITIONAL INFORMATION	Makes
Preparation Time 15 minutes, plus 2 hours chilling	**Cooking Time** 5 minutes	**Per Serving** 157 calories, 9g fat (of which 5g saturates), 17g carbohydrate, 0.3g salt	**18**

Freezing Tip

Complete the recipe and allow the cookies to cool.
Wrap, seal, label and freeze.
To use Thaw the cookies individually, as needed, at room
temperature for 1–2 hours.

Chocolate Chip Oat Cookies

125g (4oz) unsalted butter, softened, plus extra to grease

125g (4oz) golden caster sugar

1 medium egg

1 tsp vanilla extract

125g (4oz) porridge oats

150g (5oz) plain flour

1/2 tsp baking powder

200g (7oz) plain chocolate (at least 70% cocoa solids),
cut into 1cm (1/2in) chunks

1 Preheat the oven to 180°C (160°C fan oven) mark 4.
Lightly grease two baking sheets. Cream the butter
and sugar together in a bowl until pale and creamy.
Add the egg, vanilla extract and oats.

2 Sift the flour and baking powder together over the
mixture and mix until evenly combined. Stir in the
chocolate chunks.

3 Put dessertspoonfuls of the mixture on the baking
sheets, spacing them well apart to allow room for
spreading. Flatten each one slightly with the back
of a fork.

4 Bake for 12–15 minutes until risen and turning
golden, but still quite soft. Leave on the baking sheet
for 5 minutes, then transfer to a wire rack to cool.
Store in an airtight tin for up to 1 week.

Makes 18	EASY		NUTRITIONAL INFORMATION
	Preparation Time 15 minutes	**Cooking Time** 12–15 minutes, plus cooling	**Per Serving** 197 calories, 9.9g fat (of which 5.7g saturates), 26g carbohydrate, 0.2g salt

Brandy Truffles

140ml (4¹/₂fl oz) double cream

¹/₂ vanilla pod

200g (7oz) plain chocolate (at least 70% cocoa solids), broken into pieces

25g (1oz) unsalted butter, in pieces

2 tbsp brandy

25g (1oz) cocoa powder to dust

1 Pour the cream into a heavy-based pan. Split the vanilla pod and scrape the vanilla seeds into the pan, then add the pod. Slowly bring to the boil, take off the heat and set aside to infuse for 20 minutes.

2 Melt the chocolate and butter in a heatproof bowl over a pan of gently simmering water, stirring occasionally.

3 Remove the vanilla pod from the cream and discard. Stir the infused cream into the chocolate mixture, with the brandy. Pour into a shallow tin, cover and chill overnight until firm.

4 Dust your hands with cocoa powder and shape the truffle mixture into balls. Roll in cocoa to coat and put on a baking sheet lined with baking parchment. Chill overnight, or until required.

EASY	NUTRITIONAL INFORMATION	Makes
Preparation Time 35 minutes, plus overnight chilling	**Per Truffle** 100 calories, 8g fat (of which 4.6g saturates), 6.8g carbohydrate, 0.1g salt	**20**

Try Something Different

Alternatively, roll the shaped balls in 3 tbsp sifted cocoa powder, or 3 tbsp sifted golden icing sugar.

Nutty Chocolate Truffles

100g (3½oz) hazelnuts

200g (7oz) plain chocolate (minimum 50% cocoa solids), broken into pieces

25g (1oz) butter

140ml (4½fl oz) double cream

1 Put the hazelnuts into a frying pan and heat gently for 3–4 minutes, shaking the pan occasionally, to toast all over. Put 30 nuts into a bowl and leave to cool. Whiz the remaining nuts in a food processor until finely chopped or chop finely with a sharp knife. Put the chopped nuts into a shallow dish.

2 Melt the chocolate in a heatproof bowl over a pan of gently simmering water. In a separate pan, melt the butter and cream together. Bring just to the boil, then remove from the heat. Carefully stir into the chocolate. Whisk until cool and thick, then chill for 1–2 hours.

3 Put the cocoa powder and icing sugar into separate shallow dishes. Scoop up a teaspoonful of truffle mix and push a hazelnut into the centre. Working quickly, shape into a ball, then roll each ball in chopped nuts. Repeat with the remaining mix. Store in an airtight container and chill for up to two weeks.

Makes 30	EASY		NUTRITIONAL INFORMATION	
	Preparation Time 15–20 minutes, plus 1–2 hours chilling	**Cooking Time** 12 minutes, plus cooling	**Per Truffle** 96 calories, 8g fat (of which 4g saturates), 6g carbohydrate, 0.1g salt	Gluten free

Chocolate Easter Egg

275–300g (10–11oz) good-quality plain, milk or white chocolate, broken into pieces, melted (see page 10) and cooled a little, plus a little melted chocolate to assemble

ribbons and sugar flowers to decorate

1 Polish the inside of each half of a 15cm (6in) egg mould with a soft cloth. Put on a tray lined with baking parchment. Pour the melted chocolate into each half-mould, tilting gently until evenly coated. Pour any excess chocolate back into the bowl. Invert the moulds on to the baking parchment, then chill until set. Apply a second coat of chocolate, and chill again. Repeat once more, then chill for 1 hour or until set – the egg will crack if removed too soon.

2 To turn out the egg halves, trim the excess chocolate from the outer edges of the moulds, then run the point of a knife around the edge to loosen. Carefully pull each mould away from the chocolate and press firmly – the egg halves should slip out easily. Cover loosely, then chill.

3 Spread a little melted chocolate on the egg rims and, holding the other egg half in baking parchment, press on to the melted chocolate to complete the egg. Chill to set, then decorate with ribbons and sugar flowers.

A LITTLE EFFORT	NUTRITIONAL INFORMATION	Makes
Preparation Time 1 hour, plus setting	**Per Egg** 1444 calories, 80.3g fat (of which 46.5g saturates), 178.2g carbohydrate, 0.1g salt	**1**

Solid Chocolate Eggs

12 quail's eggs

450g (1lb) good-quality plain, milk or white chocolate, or a mixture of all three, broken into pieces

1 Blow the eggs to remove the yolks and whites: using a needle, pierce a tiny hole in each end of an egg and gently blow out the contents. Enlarge the hole at one end so that it's large enough to take a small piping nozzle, then wash out the shell with cold water. Leave in a warm place to dry while you blow the remaining eggs. When all the shells are completely dry, apply sticky tape over each of the tiny holes so that the chocolate won't leak out.

2 For a marbled effect, melt each type of chocolate in a separate heatproof bowl over a pan of gently simmering water. Spoon into separate nylon piping bags fitted with small, plain nozzles and pipe alternately into the shells through the larger holes, swirling the shells around from time to time to remove any air bubbles. Leave to set overnight in the refrigerator. Alternatively, use just one type of chocolate in the same way.

3 Carefully crack the eggs and peel off the shells. Wrap each chocolate egg tightly in coloured foil, then arrange in a basket.

Try Something Different

Use ordinary hen's eggs instead of quail's eggs to make larger eggs. The above quantity of chocolate is sufficient to make four of them.

Makes 12	EASY	NUTRITIONAL INFORMATION
	Preparation Time 1 hour, plus drying and setting	**Per Egg** 215 calories, 12.3g fat (of which 6.7g saturates), 24.3g carbohydrate, 0.1g salt

Cook's Tip

If you don't have a thermometer, test for the soft ball stage by dropping a teaspoon of the mixture into cold water, then rolling it between the fingers; it should form a soft ball.

Chocolate Fudge

50g (2oz) unsalted butter, plus extra to grease

225g (8oz) granulated sugar

397g can sweetened condensed milk

1 tbsp clear honey

1 tsp vanilla extract

100g (3½oz) plain chocolate (at least 70% cocoa solids), grated

1 Grease a 20.5cm (8in) square cake tin and line the base and 2.5cm (1in) up the sides with baking parchment. Put the sugar in a medium heavy-based pan and add the butter, condensed milk, honey and vanilla extract. Heat gently until the sugar dissolves. Bring to the boil, stirring, and boil for 6–8 minutes, stirring frequently to prevent sticking. The mixture is ready when it reaches the soft ball stage and registers 115°C on a sugar thermometer.

2 Remove the pan from the heat, add the grated chocolate and beat until the mixture is smooth and glossy. Pour the fudge into the prepared tin, spreading it into the corners. Leave for 2 hours or until completely set.

3 Remove the fudge from the tin and peel away the lining paper. Cut into squares. Store in an airtight container.

Makes 675g (1lb 7oz)	EASY		NUTRITIONAL INFORMATION
	Preparation Time 15 minutes	**Cooking Time** 6–8 minutes, plus cooling	**Per 25g (1oz)** 114 calories, 4g fat (of which 2.5g saturates), 19.3g carbohydrate, 0.1g salt

Index